A CENTURY
OF CHANGE
IN
GUATEMALAN
TEXTILES

This publication documents an exhibition organized by the
Center for Inter-American Relations, New York,
with the assistance of
The Textile Museum, Washington, D.C.,
for circulation to participating museums
in the United States of America.

The exhibition and publication
are supported with grants from the
BankAmerica Foundation,
National Endowment for the Arts,
a Federal Agency, Washington, D.C.,
New York State Council on the Arts,
Stanley de J. Osborne, New York,
and
INCO United States, Inc.

ANN POLLARD ROWE

A CENTURY OF CHANGE IN GUATEMALAN TEXTILES

THE CENTER FOR INTER-AMERICAN RELATIONS

Cover
Color Plate No. I
Left: Nebaj belt (detail) collected by
Lilly de Jongh Osborne (195), prob-
ably dating to the Thirties. Cotton
and silk. 8′5″x3½″ (2.57 x .09 m.)
Right: Nebaj belt (detail) collected
1967-1975. Cotton 8′4″x3⅜″ (2.54 x
.085 m.). American Museum of
Natural History 65/5910.

Inside cover
photograph ©1978 Rosalind Solomon
from the series *Guatemala*

CENTER FOR
INTER-AMERICAN RELATIONS

The Center for Inter-American Relations is a non-profit, tax-exempt
membership corporation financed by foundations, public agencies,
membership dues and corporate and individual gifts. Since its foundation in 1966, the Center has worked to help the U.S. public
broaden its awareness and appreciation of the cultural heritage of
Latin America, the Caribbean and Canada, as well as deepen its
understanding of the contemporary political, social and economic
issues confronting the Western Hemisphere.

©copyright 1981
The Center for Inter-American Relations
680 Park Avenue
New York 10021

Distributed by the
University of Washington Press,
Seattle and London

ISBN 0-295-95908-8

Library of Congress No. 81-70077

Design by Leon Auerbach
Maps by Marjorie Auerbach
Typography by Unbekant Typographers
Printed by Jaylen Lithographers Inc.
Photographs by Raymond Schwartz,
except where otherwise credited.

Contents

Preface

ROGER D. STONE
President
Center for Inter-American Relations

Not even the human and natural violence unleashed there in recent years can diminish the sheer physical beauty of Guatemala's Maya heartland. The rolling drive westward from the capital, through Indian villages and misty forest toward Lake Atitlán, remains one of the great splendors of the Americas. And the scenery is greatly enhanced by the richness and variety of the woven costumes of the region.

It has long been an ambition of the Center for Inter-American Relations to mount an exhibition of these wonderful Guatemalan costumes. But the right opportunity evaded us until 1978, when it was suggested we approach a Manhattan investment banker, Stanley de J. Osborne. Mr. Osborne's mother, the late Lilly de Jongh Osborne, had lived in Guatemala for many years and had become a keen student of the weaving tradition there. She had amassed several important collections and had written a book, *Indian Crafts of Guatemala and El Salvador*, that remains a classic source of information about the subject. After discussions, Mr. Osborne arranged to donate to the Center a large portion of his family's holdings. This collection would provide a firm basis for a definitive exhibition and catalogue.

Subsequently we were able to persuade Ann P. Rowe, the highly respected Western Hemisphere Curator at The Textile Museum in Washington, D.C., to undertake the organization of an exhibition and catalogue. Not surprisingly, we were then able to engage the interest of a variety of fine museums around the U.S. and arrange an excellent and prolonged tour for the exhibition. Many institutions and individuals have helped bring these materials to the attention of U.S. audiences. Our initial thanks must go to Mrs. Bliss Parkinson of New York, who first told us about the Osbornes, and to Mrs. Donald B. Straus, a member of the Center's Board of Directors, who relayed the suggestion

to our staff. We owe profound appreciation to Stanley Osborne and to others in his family—his sister, Elsa Ford and his brother, the late Col. Leslie B. Osborne—for the generous donations of textiles they made to the Center. Stanley Osborne additionally was kind enough to supply to the Center a financial grant that provided valuable assistance during the project's early stages. We also extend renewed thanks to INCO United States, Inc., a corporate investor in Guatemala, for their provision of an additional increment of early support.

Principal funding for the project has come from three other sources: The National Endowment for the Arts, New York State Council on the Arts and BankAmerica Foundation. Without the major assistance provided by these institutions, it would simply not have been possible to mount the exhibition and catalogue. Consolidated Edison Company of New York, Inc. has supplied most useful support for the Center's program of educational extension activities.

No less important has been the massive amount of work allocated to the project not only by Ann P. Rowe but also by a number of other professional advisers: catalogue designer Leon Auerbach, editors Judson Gooding and Celia Candlin, and photographer Raymond Schwartz. Sharon Schultz, former Deputy Director of the Center's Visual Arts program and Mara Gardner, former Education Coordinator, helped organize early stages of the project. From its outset, guidance offered by Dr. Junius Bird has been invaluable; the brief but rich Foreword he offers in this volume is an indication of the depth of his knowledge.

Finally, I must thank the current members of the Center's Visual Arts Staff: Director John Stringer, Deputy Director Kathleen Matolcsy McGuire, Education Coordinator Joan Crummer Rolland, Administrative Assistant Richard Waterman. No member of this fine team was yet working at the Center when the initial decision was made to schedule our Guatemalan exhibition. Yet all have plunged in with great energy and enthusiasm. If our exhibition and catalogue have achieved success in registering the brilliance of the weaving tradition of Guatemala, the effort of this dedicated staff is in large measure responsible.

Acknowledgements

ANN POLLARD ROWE
Curator, Western Hemisphere Textiles
The Textile Museum,
Washington, D.C.

Although the notion of tracing changes in Guatemalan textiles over the last century or so has occurred to many people, it has not been previously done in any detail. To one who has embarked upon such a project, the reason is clear enough. It requires gathering data from a multitude of different sources. Much of the written information is of limited use because it tends to generalize too much for each town, with older and newer pieces described by what they have in common rather than by their differences. No one field trip or collection suffices. One must have access both to collections, and to ethnographic photographs made over a whole succession of dates for each town to be covered. In some towns, such as Chichicastenango, sources for practically every decade are required. Few collections are complete even for a single period and no one photograph shows all details of interest. The information presented is not claimed to be definitive, but it certainly suggests avenues for further research.

For this study it has only been possible to tap the most obvious and accessible sources within the United States. More sources are known to exist. The great resources in Guatemala itself could not be examined because the time allotted for the project was relatively brief and because of the escalating violence of the current political situation there. Nevertheless, I owe much to the fact that I was able to visit Guatemala briefly in 1973 on an invitation from the Textile Committee of the Asociación Tikal, which later founded the Museo Ixchel. The trip was sponsored by the U.S. State Department (AID).

Funding for the exhibition did include travel to a number of major U.S. collections and I would like to thank the staff members of the museums involved for their courtesies, often extended under difficult conditions. These include Claudia Medoff at the University Museum, University of Pennsylvania; Lisa Whittall at the American Museum of Natural History in New York; Anna Roosevelt and Mary Jane Lenz at the Museum of the American Indian, Heye Foundation, New York; Jill Mefford, Sally Bond, Dan Jones, and Cathryn Sacra at the Peabody Museum, Harvard; E. Wyllys Andrews V, Marjorie Cengel, and Kathe Beltram at the Middle American Research Institute, Tulane University; Nora Fisher at the Museum of International Folk Art, Santa Fe; Patricia Altman at the Museum of Cultural History, UCLA; Frank Norick of the Lowie Museum of Anthropology, University of California, Berkeley. In addition, I am indebted to several private collectors who freely shared their collections and knowledge with me, not only lending items needed for illustration and exhibition but additional related textiles and photographs for study purposes. Ambassador William G. Bowdler, Ann Bowdler, Ruth Jamison, and Fifi White were all most generous. Photographers Marilyn Anderson, Susan Masuoka, and Emily Norton were similarly generous with their knowledge and materials. I am grateful to Maria de Landis of the Guatemalan Embassy for providing the photograph in Fig. 80 and for introducing me to Leonel Beteta and his wife, who also lent several items.

All of the photography, except where otherwise noted, was done by Raymond Schwartz. In general this includes photographs of textiles in the Osborne collection, The Textile Museum Collection, the Middle American Research Institute Collection, all the private collections, and Fig. 106 from The American Museum of Natural History. In addition he made the prints from all of the Tulane negatives except for Fig. 92, and the conversions from color slides to black and white prints except for Fig. 15.

The manuscript was typed by Blenda Femenias and Madelyn Miller.

Foreword

JUNIUS BIRD
Curator Emeritus
South American Archaeology
The American Museum of Natural History

The inspiration for the exhibit and this catalogue came from the availability of specimens collected by Lilly de Jongh Osborne, whose book, *Indian Crafts of Guatemala and El Salvador*, should be read by all who would like to know more about the background of the material displayed. In it are brought together the observations of a long lifetime spent in those countries, beginning in the years when traditional costumes and designs were still common, and continuing into the subsequent period of ongoing change. Through it all, her interest was not only in native textiles and costume but in all traditional crafts and, even more, in the people themselves.

I met her only once, at her home in Guatemala City. When she understood that we had called, not to try to obtain prized specimens nor to glean information for our own ends, but out of genuine interest, she was a most gracious hostess. The stories she told of her life and experiences conveyed the impression that she had never deliberately intended to form a planned collection, with all that such collecting entails. Rather she had, as occasion offered, bought the things that appealed to her esthetically or for some technical reason. To these were added purchases prompted by a desire to help some individual, or as a kindness to a friend, regardless of what was offered. Other items came as gifts. The result was a very varied, intriguing collection from which Doña Lilly, over the years, donated items to museums and to interested individuals. As an example of her generosity, some time after our visit I was surprised to receive from her a fine loom and a resist-decorated calabash. This was typical of her, for I had made no request or even hints. She had simply sensed my interest in such items and had gone to considerable trouble to get them for me.

In planning such an exhibit one could simply concentrate on the esthetically most pleasing and spectacular pieces. There is a wealth of material to draw from among existing collections and it would be tempting to do this. Such a choice, however, would not do justice to Doña Lilly's concern for the human context in which these textiles were made and used. By including complementary material from various sources Ann Rowe has brought together both earlier and later material from each of the towns included. In preparing the catalogue she has tried to provide readers with at least some information not found in the existing literature.

The many photographs of Guatemalan people wearing their costumes show them as Doña Lilly knew them and convey more vividly and accurately than any mannequin could the spirit in which the fabrics are made and used. In the exhibition the textiles are displayed flat, rather than on mannequins, allowing for full esthetic appreciation of each individual piece. It is hoped that the juxtapositions of the old and the new, of the photographs of the textiles in use and the textile itself, will create in the viewer something of the pleasure that Doña Lilly had, as well as something of her perspective, and that the exhibition and catalogue will form a fitting tribute to her long involvement with the subject.

The Highlands of Guatemala

MEXICO

● San Mateo Ixtatán

HUEHUETENANGO

Todos Santos Cuchumatán ●

■ Huehuetenango

TOTONICAPÁN

SAN MARCOS

■ Totonicapán

Salcajá ●
San Martín Sacatepéquez
● Nahualá

■ Quezaltenango

QUEZALTENANGO   *SOLOLÁ*   ■ S

L. At

San Pedro la Laguna

■Sa
A

SUCHITEPÉQUEZ

RETALHULEU

*Pacific
Ocean*

MEXICO

BELIZE

*CARIBBEAN
SEA*

GUATEMALA

HONDURAS

EL
SALVADOR

NICARAGUA

COSTA
RICA

*Pacific
Ocean*

0   10

PETÉN

ALTA VERAPAZ

● Nebaj

QUICHÉ

BAJA VERAPAZ

ZACAPA

● Chichicastenango

EL PROGRESO

CHIMALTENANGO

San Martín Jilotepeque ●

● **San Juan Sacatepéquez**

● San Pedro Sacatepéquez

● Mixco ■ Guatemala City

GUATEMALA

JALAPA

SACATEPÉQUEZ

● Palín

ESCUINTLA

JUTIAPA

SANTA ROSA

EL SALVADOR

30   40   50

MILES

● TOWNS
■ DEPARTMENT CAPITALS

CHAPTER ONE

Introduction

The portion of the modern state of Guatemala where a significant native weaving tradition has been maintained is the central and western area. This is a mountainous zone with an average elevation of 4,000 feet, although there are peaks as high as 10,000 feet. The climate is temperate, with dry and rainy seasons. In the west, in the Department of Huehuetenango are the rugged Cuchumatanes Mountains, where the highest elevations are found. To the south is a series of active volcanoes, which separates the highlands from the tropical Pacific coastal zone. In the shadows of these volcanoes in the central highlands is Lake Atitlán, at an altitude of 5,100 feet. The land is green and of spectacular natural beauty. Its broken character makes it more suitable for traditional native methods of agriculture than for European methods, and thus has contributed to the preservation of other aspects of native culture as well.

Linguistically the people are Maya, a large language category which includes a number of related, but not necessarily mutually intelligible, languages.[1] In the central highlands Quiché, Cakchiquel and Tzutujil are closely related to each other and are mutually intelligible to some extent. The Kekchian group, which consists of Kekchi and Pocomchi in the northern area of Alta Verapaz and Pocomám to the east, is distinct. Even farther removed from the Quiché group are the languages found in the western highlands. The most important of these is Mam, to which Ixil is also related. Kanhobal and Chuj are also distinct. Still other Mayan languages are found in parts of southern Mexico.

Historical Background
The historical relation of highland Guatemala to the areas of the Maya high culture, which flourished in the lowland tropical forests of the Petén in the so-called Classic Period (c. A.D. 300-1000) and in the Yucatan in the Postclassic Period (A.D. 1000-1524), is not entirely clear. Certainly there is lowland Maya influence in the highlands. There is also Mexican influence of various kinds. But the area seems mostly to have been a provincial backwater that was on the receiving end of influences, rather than sending out influences of its own or participating fully in the more spectacular cultures of neighboring regions. For all that, it is today, together with the neighboring highlands of Chiapas, the site of the most extensive and interesting

survival of pre-conquest native traditions in the Maya area.

In the time immediately preceding the Spanish conquest, which was initiated by Pedro de Alvarado in 1524, the Guatemalan highlands consisted of a number of small warring kingdoms, partly corresponding to the different language groups and partly subdivisions of these (such as Sacatepéquez). Although they were unable to unite against Alvarado, they fought desperately and conquest was achieved only with great cruelty and widespread slaughter.

Spanish culture had its greatest impact in the first few decades after the conquest. The elite and ruling members of the native kingdoms were simply killed off. The Spanish then established encomiendas, in which large tracts of land together with their native residents were given by the Spanish crown to their conquerors, a practice that was subject to so many abuses that in 1542 restrictive laws were enacted. The Spanish also tried to consolidate the population into towns laid out in Spanish style on a grid system and with a central plaza and church. Conversion of the native population to Catholicism was given as high a priority as was the search for gold—of which there was actually very little in Guatemala. Conversion, however, was not complete, and in many towns remnants of old beliefs and religious customs still survive, in some cases separate from, and in other cases blended with, Catholic rituals. New domestic animals, such as sheep, chickens, and horses, and new food crops, were also introduced.

In 1720 the encomiendas were abolished and there was a relaxation of Spanish control. Political independence from Spain, declared in 1821, had little effect on the economic and social order under which the native people lived. Far greater social and economic change resulted from the establishment of a coffee export industry in the late 19th century, since Indian labor was required on the large plantations.[2] Many Indians leave their mountain communities for a few months of seasonal labor each year in the Pacific coastal zone. It has meant on the one hand the end of the comparative isolation from Ladino society which had previously prevailed in some areas, since it was at this time that Ladinos moved into many previously all-Indian towns as labor recruiters and entrepreneurs. On the other hand, it has meant the gradual erosion of the predominantly self-sustaining economic pattern based on subsistence agriculture. A vicious cycle was created, where labor exodus (at first forced) and land appropriation (for the plantations) make it necessary for some Indians to buy food with cash, which they receive as wages for working on the plantations. Buying food with cash allows for population increases in a situation where there was already insufficient land to support everyone in the traditional way, so that to get food for the extra mouths, additional people must go to work for wages.

Since World War II this process has been accelerated by further population increases—some due to improved health services—and there are a number of other pressures which threaten traditional life styles. When an Indian must leave his village to take wage labor, there is tremendous social pressure to abandon native customs and clothing, which may be ridiculed out of their usual context. The construction of roads and the advance of rural education have also brought increased contacts with European culture. Protestant missionary work has had some impact, causing the breakdown of Catholic institutions like the cofradías (see below), in which native elements had become so deeply integrated, that a significant component of traditional belief and practice is lost with them. Damage from the earthquake of 1976 has also had a substantial disrupting influence on traditional life styles.

It is not, however, with the breakdown of native tradition that this exhibition and catalogue are concerned, but rather with some of its most colorful and still vital aspects. A few words should therefore be said about associated cultural forms, in order to place the weaving in its context.

The traditional means of subsistence is agriculture, with maize the most important crop. Maize cultivation is accompanied by rituals and is of a religious and psychological importance in addition to its value as food. Other native plants that are extensively grown are beans and squash. The methods and tools of cultivation are likewise of pre-conquest origin. Agricultural work is done primarily by men; women do the cooking, child-rearing, weaving and pottery-making. Goods not produced at home are acquired in the market system. Most towns have a market in the main plaza at least once a week. People come from other towns to buy and sell.

Although the basic cultural unit is the village, not everyone lives in a house in the town itself. Many live out in the surrounding countryside, coming into town mainly for market, Catholic religious observances, and fiestas. Towns vary somewhat from each other in their dispersal pattern. Often the people who

live further out of town are more conservative culturally than those in town. In each town there is also a small group of Ladinos, people of whatever descent who follow a European value system and way of life. These people consider themselves socially superior to the native population and are in turn resented by the Indians, but interdependence and coexistence have been the general pattern.

The local civil and religious hierarchies have grown up from a combination of Spanish and native elements. There is a graded system of public offices related to age and wealth. Holding office is costly so that the system by its nature tends to hold down the absolute accumulation of wealth. The religious hierarchy is organized by means of cofradías, or confraternaties, which are guardians of the images or standards of the saints and which organize and finance the community's holy day celebrations. Larger towns have several cofradías. Some native elements are often included in these observances. The more important members of the cofradías may have special costumes that they wear for the processions of the saints.

Beyond these basic similarities of life there is considerable differentiation between villages, making the Guatemalan highlands an anthropologically rich area within a remarkably small compass. Besides language, which has already been mentioned, and costumes, which are the subject of this catalogue, there are many other detailed differences: in religious practices; in house and pottery types; in methods of carrying goods; and in specialized production, with certain towns producing a specific type of decorated gourd or tule mat, for example.

Textile History
At the outset it must be admitted that very little is known about either weaving or costume of the Guatemalan highlands before the late 19th century. For the lowland Maya, evidence of familiarity with textiles is found both in pictorial representations and in actual fabrics, although specimens of the latter are small and poorly preserved.[3] But for the highlands, the only specific traces for most of the area's history are clay spindle whorls, and impressions of coarse plain-weave textiles on pottery. This evidence allows us to say that they did indeed spin and weave, probably cotton, but that is all. The spindle whorls first appear in Middle Preclassic times (600-300 B.C.), later than the first use of pottery, which occurs in the Early Preclassic. Also from Middle and Late Preclassic times are figurines depicting women wearing knee-length skirts and men with loincloths. It has been suggested that cotton was introduced from LaVenta, on the Gulf Coast of Mexico, the center of late Olmec culture,

along with more specifically indentifiable traits from this area.[4] In the Early Classic Period (A.D. 300-700), which is characterized by extensive influence from Teotihuacán in Mexico, the only representations show people in elaborate ceremonial gear that probably bore little relation to everyday clothing. In Late Classic times (A.D. 700-1000) after the fall of Teotihuacán, there are representations of figures wearing loincloths, belts, capes, huipils of net-like material, and sandals. There are, however, virtually no representations of costumes from Post-classic times until the Spanish conquest.

The scanty evidence cited above does suggest, however, that weaving and costume followed general Mesoamerican practices, which are documented pictorially and in a few actual textile fragments for lowland Maya and other nearby areas. In addition, there are a few passing references to pre-conquest garment types in some Spanish colonial accounts. It is probably safe to assume that weaving was done on the backstrap loom, that cloth was made to the exact size and shape required for a specific purpose (or a simple fraction thereof), and that fabrics were worn draped. These features all are in direct contrast to European textile and costume traditions, in which the treadle loom was used to weave yardage which was then cut and shaped to fit the form of the body or some fanciful variation thereof.

The loincloth and cape were the principal items of masculine attire in highland Guatemala at the time of Spanish contact, according to research by Patricia Rieff Anawalt, possibly supplemented by a triangular hipcloth and the xicolli, a sleeveless jacket-like garment.[5] Women wore a wrapped skirt and a huipil, a

simple tunic-like upper body garment. Huipil is a Nahuatl (Aztec) word, but it is now frequently used for this garment wherever it appears in Mesoamerica. Two different Colonial sources describe the Guatemalan huipil as being worn loosely over the skirt, the same way it was worn by other Mesoamerican groups.[6] For some reason, while the male costume is similar to that of the lowland Maya of the same period, the female costume is completely different.

Unfortunately, there is also a dearth of information on textile innovations and costume changes of the Colonial period. When the lacuna ends and information becomes available for the late 19th century, it is clear that the male costume had been almost completely changed but that the female costume retained many pre-conquest elements. The only way to date these changes is by comparison with dated European antecedents. Unfortunately, few such antecedents are datable; some appear to have been derived from Spanish peasant dress, which in itself is poorly documented. It is probable that changes occurred throughout this time span.

Innovations affecting textiles generally include the introduction of sheep, and of the treadle loom. These new elements are found alongside of native weaving practices in many areas. They represent additions to the repertory, rather than substitutions. The treadle loom functions in a totally different context than does the native backstrap loom. While the backstrap loom is most often employed by women who use it primarily to weave clothes for their families and who limit themselves to cotton almost exclusively, the treadle loom is used by men to produce both wool and cotton fabric commercially. The commer-

Nebaj market, 1979. Photograph by Emily Norton. Black and white from color original.

15

cial context of treadle loom weaving is as much a carry-over from its European use which was similarly commercial, as is the loom itself.

Modern Costume Repertory

The woman's costume still consists of a wrapped skirt and a huipil. The huipil is usually made of two pieces of fabric woven on the backstrap loom and then joined along their side selvedges with the seams worn vertically, although one-piece and three-piece examples also occur. On the huipil is lavished the greatest skill of the weaver, and thus the Guatemalan huipil is the most artistically interesting as well as the most readily recognized item of native apparel. Huipils made in a single town often vary from one another in the amount of decoration woven into them. Completely unpatterned huipils are made and worn in many towns along side of those with lavish supplementary-weft decoration. In some towns a huipil different from the everyday one is worn for cofradía functions (see for example those from San Juan Sacatepéquez and Nahualá in Chapters Three and Five). The cofradía huipil is not necessarily more lavish than the everday huipil; in fact, as in Santiago Atitlán and Chichicastenango (Chapters Four and Six) it may be less so. It appears, in the cases where one can trace it, to follow a more conservative form than the daily huipil.

Although the huipil is a completely native form, it has in fact been subject to some European influences. One of these is the manner in which it is worn. Except where it is worn very short (Palín, Alta Verapaz), the huipil is usually tucked into the skirt, instead of hanging loose as appears to have been the case in pre-conquest times. Exceptions to this practice are found, however, in Chuj (San Mateo Ixtatán, Chapter Twelve), and Kanhobal costume (both in the remote northern area of Huehuetenango), and in the manner of wearing cofradía huipils, which are put on over the regular clothing.

Another possible European influence is embroidery around the neckline—decoration added with a needle after the fabric is taken from the loom. In some cases, for instance Quezaltenango, the European influence is obvious (Chapter Eight). In other instances, as in the huipils from Santiago Atitlán, Nebaj or Chichicastenango, it is not so clear. In the case of San Mateo Ixtatán, the original source of the embroidery may have been European, but its present exuberance is clearly an indigenous development. In a few instances, huipil fabric is woven on treadle looms, sometimes imitating European designs, as in Quezaltenango, and sometimes imitating native weaving, as in some Totonicapán examples.

Skirt fabrics, on the other hand, are usually woven commercially on treadle looms, although there are exceptions (Aguacatán and some Mam villages in Huehuetenango). There are two especially common types. The more conservative is of indigo-dyed cotton, usually with light weft or warp-and-weft stripes. The second type, which is supplanting the first in quite a few villages, has weft or warp-and-weft ikat patterning. Ikat patterning is formed by tie-dyeing the yarns of the fabric before they are woven. Although it is possible to create complex patterns by this method, the technique is used in relatively simple form in Guatemala. The origin of the indigo plaids may possibly derive from native forms, but the origin of the ikat patterning is more problematic and may be a post-conquest introduction. The principal center for ikat dyeing and weaving is the Ladino village of Salcajá, near Quezaltenango. Both types of skirt fabric may be worn either wrapped in native fashion or gathered in European fashion (e.g., Quezaltenango). There are a variety of ways of wrapping the skirt, either with or without a belt, depending on the village. Usually the fabric must be pieced to some extent, with two lengths of fabric sewn together side to side. This rectangle is worn with the seam horizontal, and usually the ends are sewn together to form a tube. Sometimes this stitching is simply done on a sewing machine, but in other villages the work is done by hand, using colorful threads and large stitches in order to create a decorative effect (San Juan Sacatepéquez, Chichicastenango). Such a seam is called a randa (a Spanish word).

Belts, by which are meant comparatively narrow and stiff items, and sashes, by which are meant relatively broad and flexible ones, are normally backstrap-loom woven. Some belts and most sashes are locally made and correspond in style to other items woven in the village. Others are commercially produced and widely marketed. One type of belt of relatively wide distribution has black and white lengthwise stripes, either all in wool, or in a combination of wool and cotton. They are woven by men in the Chichicastenango area and sold to different villages, where they are often embroidered in a local style (cf. Chichicastenango examples) but sometimes left plain (cf. San Martín Sacatepéquez).

Women usually wear some type of ribbon in their hair. Most frequently, this consists of strips of machine-made fabric braided with the hair into two plaits, sometimes left hanging down the back and sometimes pinned up into a coronet on the head. A number of villages use handwoven, though commercially produced, ribbons made in Totonicapán. These

Children from San Martín Sacatepéquez. Their clothing is identical to that of adults (see chapter 9), only woven to their smaller size. Photograph by Emily Norton, 1978; black and white from color original.

are made on very simple treadle looms, and often have tapestry patterns, in which the colored wefts (the threads that cross the warp) turn back at the edges of each color area. Various geometric and animal patterns are used. These ribbons vary in length, depending on the village where they are worn and the inclinations of the individual woman. They are added to the hair in various ways. In a few villages the ribbons are locally woven, and these often give an extraordinary effect (cf. Nebaj and Palín).

Women's shawls vary from square cloths, which seem to be native in type, to oblong, fringed rectangles related to the rebozo. The origin of the rebozo is obscure but it definitely seems to be a post-conquest form. Since rebozos in Guatemala as well as in Mexico, Ecuador, and Peru, are often ikat-patterned, it is possible that the two items entered the textile repertory of the New World at the same time. The similarity of the designs used in the places where a rebozo-like form is now found indicates a relationship between these areas which is very unlikely to have grown up in pre-conquest times, especially since the rebozo form does not resemble known pre-conquest textiles in any of these areas.

The terminology is not entirely consistent, but the item is usually called a tzute if square or a perraje if rectangular and fringed. They perform the same functions, however. The cloth may be folded on the head as a sunshade, or used as a sling to carry a baby, or for a shawl. When not in use, it is often draped over one shoulder. A variety of sizes may be made in a particular town, especially if locally woven. Smaller ones may be used to cover the contents of baskets, or to wrap around ceremonial paraphernalia, such as candles carried in procession, so that the hands do not touch the object.

Another type of small textile whose function overlaps that of the small tzute is usually called servilleta, the Spanish word for napkin. This word is convenient to use if in fact the item is distinguishable in form from the tzute. In towns where this is the case, such as Palín (Chapter Two), the tzute usually has four finished edges while the servilleta has fringed ends. The servilleta may also have a predominantly white coloring, which contrasts with the bright color of the tzute. Not all villages have a distinctive hand-made servilleta. Commercial fabrics may also be substituted for the purposes for which a servilleta is normally used.

The modern Guatemalan man's costume follows the general European tradition of shirt and pants plus various types of accessories, but there is considerable variation from one village to another in the degree of acculturation. In some villages the Indian male costume is indistinguishable from that of the Ladinos and no vestige of native tradition remains. In others, the cloth is commercially produced, but cut and sewn in an archaic style that is distinct from modern clothing but is not really native either. The Chichicastenango man's costume is the most interesting of these (Chapter Six). In a few towns the man's shirt and pants are made by sewing backstrap-loom woven rectangles together. Usually a broad sash is worn with handwoven pants or pants of archaic cut. These sashes are usually backstrap-loom woven. Also worn in some towns, are headscarves, often from backstrap looms, which are usually called tzutes, but their use has been steadily declining. A European style hat may be added to or substituted for the tzute.

To provide additional warmth, a variety of wool overgarments are found whose source is not readily explainable; they may be the results of a combination of native and European influences. A small rectangular hip cloth, often called by the Spanish term rodillera, is worn in a number of the lake villages and in Nahualá (Chapter Five). Overpants split to the thigh are another such garment. They are rare in everyday dress today, Todos Santos being the outstanding exception (Chapter Ten), but they were common in ceremonial dress in earlier times, for example in Totonicapán (Chapter Seven). Various types of jackets of obvious European derivation are common,

some of archaic cut and some of a more modern style. An alternative upper body overgarment is the capixay; the word is of Spanish derivation and the garment embodies European features (most notably nonfunctional sleeves), but its actual prototype is unclear. The capixay is a narrow garment, usually mid-thigh to knee length, which is pulled on over the head. It may or may not be sewn up the sides. The San Martín Sacatepéquez costume illustrates the use of this garment (Chapter Nine).

The Loom

The backstrap loom (sometimes also called a stick loom) is an ingenious and simple device (see illustration). It is native to the Americas, and was used from ancient times throughout Mesoamerica. It consists simply of the *warp*, the longitudinal threads of the cloth to be woven, and a series of sticks which facilitate the insertion of the *weft*, or transverse threads. The warp is made the exact size wanted for the finished piece, and the size of the various loom parts more or less conforms to the size of the warp.

Santa Catarina Palopó woman weaving on the backstrap loom. The backstrap is clearly visible above her feet. The end of the front loom bar can be seen below her right elbow. A second bar has been placed next to it to facilitate rolling up the length of cloth already woven. She is inserting the weft into the shed created by the heddle rod and held open by the sword which has been placed on edge. The sword is the stick just above her right hand and the heddle rod is next, followed by the shed rod. The warp cross can be seen between the shed rod and heddle rod. The smaller stick above is a supplementary shed rod used to assist in creating a shed for the supplementary wefts. The last stick is the lease stick, placed in the same shed as the heddle rod. Photograph by the author, 1973; black and white from color original.

The two wooden sticks to which the warp is attached are generally referred to as *loom bars* (see also Fig. 36).

The warp passes continuously from one loom bar to the other without being cut. Usually the warp does not pass around the loom bars but around a yarn or cord commonly referred to as a *heading cord* (Fig. 36). This heading cord is held in place against the loom bar by a lashing spiralling around both the cord and the bar. The cord may be several strands of the weft used in the rest of the fabric, or a separate cord that can be withdrawn on completion of the weaving. In either case, the result is a warp end selvedge. Whether or not the actual heading cord remains in the fabric, the first few wefts that are inserted are often doubled or tripled and can be referred to as the heading.

Separating the warp yarns in order to pass the weft through is referred to as forming a *shed*, the shed being the space through which the weft is passed. For plain weave, the even-numbered warps and the odd-numbered warps need to be raised alternately since in *plain weave*, the weft passes over-one and under-one warp in each passage, reversing the over-under order from one passage to the next. For the passage of one weft, the even-numbered warps are raised above the odd-numbered ones, and for the passage of the next weft, the positions of these two layers are reversed. This basic interchange of the two layers of warps is referred to as the warp cross. This cross is most clearly visible in a side view of the weaving (see accompanying photograph).

In backstrap looms, a single stick controls each of the two layers. To form one shed every other warp is picked up and a round stick referred to as the *shed rod* is inserted, thus raising the layer of warps passing over it and lowering the layer passing under it. The other shed is made by means of another stick, the *heddle rod*, which is placed in front of the shed rod. The heddle rod is attached to every other warp by a cord which passes alternately around one of the warps underneath the shed rod, and then over the heddle rod. Each loop enclosing a warp is a heddle. The loops must be long enough so that when the heddle rod is resting on the warps the layer passing over the shed rod may still be raised. To raise the warps controlled by the heddle rod, the rod is lifted (usually with the shed rod pushed back out of the way). To raise the other layer of warps, those which pass over the shed rod, the heddle rod is allowed to rest on the warps and the shed rod is moved forward. Since the shed rod and heddle rod are applied to the warp after it is wound on the loom bars, the warps do not need to be cut as they are in European style treadle looms in which the warp ends are passed through a fixed apparatus.

The remaining tools used for weaving may be

Todos Santos woman weaving on the backstrap loom. The ragged backstrap, front loom bar, and sword are the only parts of the loom visible. Her huipil is in the latest style, virtually covered with discontinuous weft patterning. Photograph by Emily Norton, 1979; black and white from color original.

briefly described. The *sword* or *batten* is a flat stick of hard wood, usually pointed at both ends, which is used to aid in opening the shed, in holding the shed open for the insertion of the weft and in beating the weft into place after it is inserted. Beyond the shed rod is another smaller stick called a *lease stick* which passes through the same shed as the heddle rod. It helps to hold the warps in order, although it does not function actively in the weaving. The weft yarn is wound on a narrow stick called a *shuttle*. The length of the shuttle is equivalent to the width of the warp. The weft yarn is wound lengthwise on the shuttle, and around the stick at the ends.

A device for maintaining the warp tension is essential to the effective separation of the warps in forming sheds and for beating in the weft. The backstrap serves this purpose. The far end of the loom is secured with a rope to a house post or other convenient support, while the end of the loom nearest the weaver is affixed to a strong broad strap which passes around the weaver's hips. The weaver merely leans back to increase tension on the warp and forward to decrease the tension.

The backstrap loom can produce a fabric with four finished selvedges, unlike the treadle loom, which produces fabrics with side selvedges only, since the warps must be cut in order to pass through the heddles. The heddles are a fixed part of the treadle loom apparatus, and are not removable as they are on the backstrap loom. The fabric woven on a backstrap loom is not cut when it is removed from the loom although it may be folded or seamed to another piece. The entire warp length is woven and as the length of unwoven warp decreases, it becomes more difficult to manipulate the shed rod, heddle rod and sword. At first a smaller shed rod and sword are substituted, but eventually all these devices must be removed. The wefts must then be inserted into the remaining unwoven warp with large needles. This is as difficult and time-consuming a process as it sounds, and it is not easy to make it match the rest of the weaving. This area where the weaving is finished can be referred to as the area of terminal construction, or simply as the terminal area. In plain-woven fabrics the wefts are often not as closely spaced in this terminal area as in the rest of the weaving. In some Guatemalan towns, however, it has become the practice not to do the terminal weaving and instead to cut the warps at one end or to put a double length of warp on the loom and cut it in the middle. Such a fabric has three selvedges and the fourth edge is simply hemmed (e.g., Palín, San Martín Sacatepéquez huipils, Chichicastenango tzutes).

Most fabrics woven on the backstrap loom in Guatemala are plain weave, usually with the warps more closely spaced than the wefts. If the warps are so closely spaced that the weft does not show on the surface of the fabric, it is described as warp-faced.

The usual method of patterning the fabrics is with supplementary wefts. These extra wefts are added to the fabric alternately with the ground weft. If the supplementary wefts turn at the edges of small design areas instead of extending continuously from selvedge to selvedge, the technique is often referred to as *brocading*. A variety of methods of inserting supplementary wefts are used in Guatemalan weaving, each town, again, being distinctive. For instance, supplementary wefts may be inserted with the plain-weave shed open or closed. If the plain-weave shed is closed (with the batten lying on its side), the supplementary weft will usually pass to the back of the fabric when it is not being used on the front, whereas if the plain-weave shed is open (with the batten turned on edge as illustrated, p. 18), the supplementary weft will pass in the same shed as the ground weft where it does not appear on the front. In the first instance, a negative image of the pattern will appear on the back of the fabric, while in the second, no patterning at all will be visible on the back if the textile is warp-faced.

Since the ground fabrics are usually warp-faced, the supplementary weft normally passes over several warps on the front of the fabric, in what is referred to as a *float*. Sometimes the length of the floats in a textile is uniform and characteristic and can be expressed either by means of the interlacing order —for example, 3/1, which means that the supplementary weft passes over three warps and under one,—or by describing simply the float span. For example, a 3-span float is a float that passes over three warps. It is assumed that the supplementary weft passes under one warp between floats unless otherwise specified.

If the design is made up of small elements, the length and arrangement of the floats is dependent on the design. For larger designs, where there is a regular arrangement of floats of uniform length, the alignment of the floats is also important to note. It may be *alternating*, in which the floats are staggered from one row to the next, like brickwork; *vertical*, in which the floats appear directly above each other in columns, or *diagonal*, in which the floats are offset one warp in each succeeding row, forming diagonal ribs.

Other features that may be noted include how a discontinuous supplementary weft is turned at the edges of the design as it is carried from one shed to the next. For instance, it may be carried on the front or the back; or one end of the yarn may be inserted to begin, or the middle of the yarn may be put under the warps to begin, in which case the two ends cross each other in opposite directions in succeeding sheds. Sometimes the supplementary weft, instead of passing over and under succeeding warps, actually wraps all the way around the warps. In Guatemalan textiles, this wrapping technique is used mainly for narrow diagonal or vertical columns of design.

In addition, there are variations in the processes used to insert supplementary wefts, even among villages where the finished effect of the weaving might be similar. Sometimes the supplementary wefts are simply inserted with the fingers. Sometimes a thin stick, referred to as a pick-up stick, is used to separate the warps over and under which the supplementary wefts are to be passed. If the float lengths are to be uniform, a supplementary shed rod and sometimes extra heddle rods, may be added to the loom, controlling the warps under which the supplementary wefts pass. In such cases, however, the weaver must still select those warps needed for the particular design she desires to weave.

This kind of weaving, being direct and not mechanical, allows for close artistic control over the results. Although not all weavers attain results of high artistic quality, the possibility is always there, and it is sometimes realized. The insertion of supplementary wefts on such textiles is a very time consuming process. It is not uncommon for it to take ten minutes to arrange the supplementary wefts for a single shed of the ground weave. To complete a particularly elaborate piece, a weaver might take six months, although this would also include time spent on household chores. Weaving is one of the world's slowest ways of creating art, a fact not easily appreciated by those of us who are accustomed to simple machine-made fabrics in our daily lives. Even in our culture, most hand weavers use the treadle loom, which is capable of much greater speed than the backstrap loom, although the artistic potential is also significantly reduced.

The treadle loom is designed for speed and is therefore more suitable for commercial production than the backstrap loom. To change the shed, the weaver simply presses on a treadle with his foot and the shed is cleared instantly, without the need to insert a sword or strum the warps, as is required on the backstrap loom. His hands are free to simply throw the shuttle, and beat in the weft. The shuttle is a two-part affair, consisting of a small bobbin on which the weft is wound, set into a smooth box open on one side. As the box passes through the shed the weft automatically unwinds from the bobbin. The weaver causes the shuttle to slide across the warps with a flick of one wrist. The shuttle is caught with the other hand. The beater on a treadle loom is built in. It consists of a framework of metal slats through which the warps pass. It is set on pivots, so the weaver merely draws it forward with a jerk to beat down each weft. Alternately throwing the shuttle and beating, a treadle loom weaver can weave some 60-90 wefts per minute of plain weave. This time may be compared to two wefts per minute of plain weave, which is a typical speed on a backstrap loom.[7] Another way time is saved in treadle-loom weaving is in setting up the loom. For commercial production, very long lengths of warp are put on the loom, enough, for example, for thirty skirts, whereas in back-strap loom weaving, the loom is set up separately for each item, and a single garment may even require two or three setups which can easily take five hours each, to which can be added another two hours for the terminal weaving on a four-selvedge fabric. It should be emphasized, however, that the textural and artistic qualities of fabrics woven on the backstrap loom are much superior to those woven on treadle looms, and it is with such textiles that this catalogue is chiefly concerned.

Descriptive Approach

It has only been over the last hundred years or so that anyone has attempted to record or collect Guatemalan textiles. The earlier records were made by people who were in Guatemala for some other purpose, such as archaeology or missionary work, and who were struck by the beauty and strong regional distinctiveness of the native costumes. Early observers and collectors included the Maudslays, whose book was published in 1899, and whose small textile collection is now in the Victoria and Albert Museum, London; Dr. Gustavus Eisen, who was in Guatemala in 1902 and whose collection is at the Lowie Museum of Anthropology, University of California at Berkeley and was included in O'Neale's study; Father Henry T. Heyde, who left Guatemala in 1895 and whose collection is now at the American Museum of Natural History, New York; and George Byron Gordon, whose photographs and a few textiles are at the Peabody Museum, Harvard. These collections, while of great importance, are sometimes difficult to work with. Although Father Heyde seems to have understood village variations in

San Martín Sacatepéquez woman winding a warp in preparation for weaving. Women weave for their families during the time not spent on or in combination with other domestic duties. Photograph by Emily Norton, 1978; black and white from color original.

costume himself, he supplied no documentation to the American Museum for his collection. The Gordon photographs are also undocumented. Eisen's collection has generally accurate village documentation, but it includes, as do most other collections of this vintage, a large proportion of commercial treadle-loom woven fabrics from Quezaltenango, Totonicapán, and Huehuetenango, and a relatively small proportion of the more interesting backstrap-loom woven materials.

In the 1920s Guatemala was visited by the anthropologists Samuel K. Lothrop and Oliver LaFarge. La Farge worked in the Department of Huehuetenango and was principally interested in archaeology and modern belief systems, but he made some records of costume for a few towns (see San Mateo Ixtatán). The textiles he acquired are now at The Middle American Research Institute, Tulane University. Lothrop made several visits to Guatemala, in the Teens, Twenties and Thirties, and the textiles he acquired are now at the Peabody Museum, Harvard, Museum of the American Indian, New York, and the Lowe Art Museum, Miami.

The 1930s saw a great burst of collecting activity. The collection made by Matilda Geddings Gray, now at Tulane, includes a large number of complete costumes and is uniquely valuable among U.S. collections in this respect. Unfortunately, these have never been properly published, although O'Neale included them in her study and a small catalogue was issued in 1976. Lila O'Neale was in Guatemala in 1936 and her study is the most comprehensive on the subject. She was a trained anthropologist for whom textiles, instead of being a sideline, were her principal interest. That fact is reflected in the wealth of information the book contains. Her data base included not only her own collection (now at the Lowie Museum) but also Eisen's material, the Gray collection at Tulane, and the Mildred Palmer collection now at the Museo Ixchel, Guatemala City. Even so, there are gaps and even a few errors, quite apart from the fact that the book is hopelessly underillustrated.

About this time Lilly de Jongh Osborne was also active. She began publishing articles in the late Twenties and wrote a small book which appeared in 1935, the first work of more than a few pages on the subject of Guatemalan textiles (O'Neale's did not appear until 1945).[8] She continued collecting and writing and a longer book appeared in 1965. Collections she made were acquired by the University Museum in Philadelphia in 1942 and by the Smithsonian Institution in 1966. These collections are not systematic, but they certainly include interesting material. The present work draws principally upon the collection she

had at the time of her death in 1975. Some of the pieces are illustrated in her own publications, and others are newer. Her interest in Guatemalan textiles was lifelong, and living in the country gave her unequalled access to the material. Nevertheless, her book, like O'Neale's, is underillustrated.

In the late Thirties and Forties a number of people interested in Guatemalan costumes made sets of color renderings. Those of Josephine Wood and Frederick Crocker were published in color and are especially noteworthy. The more recent watercolors of Carmen Petterson are in the same tradition. The use of colored drawings for this purpose was of course a response to the lack of adequate color photographic technique at that time, always excepting *The National Geographic Magazine,* which published several articles before 1950 using black and white photographs which had been carefully tinted. These color drawings are valuable, but have the severe limitation that the texture or fabric structure of the cloth cannot be represented. Actual errors, such as incorrectly draping the garments or combining garments of different dates, can occur if the artist dresses models in textiles from someone's collection, rather than simply recording what the people in the village happen to be wearing at the time of a visit. Since Wood's drawings were made by the latter method, they provide the most valuable record. It should be noted that the same possibility of error exists with the use of non-native models in photography, and for that reason the present book is illustrated only with ethnographic photographs and with photographs of textiles laid out flat.

Among the most valuable of recent publications redressing the comparative lack of photographic documentation of Guatemalan textiles are the works of Anderson (1978) and of Sperlich (1980). They have concentrated on recording the specific weaving techniques used in the different villages, an aspect of the subject almost totally neglected previously except by O'Neale, who gave it rather summary treatment.

The subject of Guatemalan textiles is still far from adequately documented. In truth, it is too vast for any single volume. There are over 150 towns in which a distinctive costume has been worn at least until the last 100 years or so for which documentation and examples are available. In many of these towns, a large variety of items has been produced, for men's, women's, and children's wear, and for everyday and ceremonial use. The ways in which each item is made and the ways in which it is used are of interest, in each town. The textiles have not remained static with time, either: there have been many kinds of changes over the past hundred years. Not all of these changes in-

Santiago Atitlán woman spinning cotton. Her huipil is embroidered. Photograph by Emily Norton, 1978; black and white from color original.

volve the simple adoption of modern European style clothing; some are related to the availability of certain types of materials or to design influences, and they are within the native technical tradition.

Most of the earlier publications have tended to treat many towns superficially or with only a relatively narrow focus. This volume takes the opposite approach. The number of towns selected was kept relatively small, in order to permit providing some depth of coverage for each. The overall textile repertory, the manner of wearing the costume, the textile structures and weaving techniques are considered, as well as the principal observable changes. The selection of towns was based in part on the availability of older and newer photographs and specimens, as well as on

the strengths of the Osborne collection, so that the list is a familiar one. Even so, the format makes possible the presentation of previously unpublished data in every case. The old black-and-white photographs, even though flawed in technique and by time, contain much valuable information; they are a resource that should be explored further. The opportunity has also been taken to publish some of the fine older textiles in color.

Following the discussion of each town is a list of major published references. The compilation of such lists was essential to this study and it is hoped that they may also be useful to others. They can be considered supplementary to the notes and illustrations provided here. The entries are grouped first according to the kind of information they provide: ethnographic photographs; explication of weaving techniques; textiles photographed flat or on models as opposed to showing them in context; colored renderings of people in costumes; drawings, usually of individual textiles; texts which include information not found in the accompanying illustrations; and finally, anthropological background material, if available. In all categories except that of colored renderings, the illustrations are in black and white unless otherwise specified. In the text category, the references are primarily to O'Neale's costume descriptions, and Delgado's dissertation, the original of which was fully illustrated but which is generally available only in Xerox form, in which only the drawings reproduce well. The individual entries are listed chronologically in order of publication, although in some cases the material illustrated is significantly older than the date of publication. For instance, Wood's color drawings were made in 1939 to 1942, but were not published until 1966. In some cases the source of the photographs is given in order to indicate the date; for example, for O'Neale's illustrations of Eisen's 1902 specimens as opposed to pieces from the Thirties. In some cases, an illustration is listed which is unidentified, or wrongly identified, in its original source.

Changes

Before proceeding to particular examples, a few further words can be said about some of the general types of changes that Guatemalan textiles have undergone in the past century. Of these, the most important involves the availability of different types of materials.

Originally, Guatemalan textiles were woven of handspun cotton yarns dyed with natural dyes, the most important of which were indigo, cochineal red, and shellfish purple. The process of handspinning is extremely time consuming. The cotton has first to be deseeded and fluffed up, usually by beating it on a pad with sticks.[9] Then it can be drawn out and twisted into thread. The native tool for this process in Guatemala is a simple spindle, consisting of a wooden stick with a spherical or disc-shaped whorl of clay (or wood) near one end, which serves to steady the spindle as it turns. One end rests on the ground or in a gourd or clay bowl, and the spinner twirls the other end with her fingers. She holds the unspun fibers in her other hand. The tip ends of these unspun fibers are twisted onto previously spun thread at the top of the spindle. As the spindle is turned, she draws out the fibers with her other hand. The turning of the spindle causes this new length of thread to twist, and it is the twist that imparts strength to the thread. When an arm's length of thread has been produced, she has to stop and wind it onto

the spindle and then begin again. A speed of about 11'8" (3.56m.) per minute has been recorded for this type of cotton spinning in Guatemala.[10] Yarn preparation can easily take as long as the actual weaving of a plain weave fabric on the backstrap loom. There are two distinct species of cotton in Guatemala: a long-staple white cotton (Gossypium hirsutum) and a shorter-staple tawny-colored cotton (Gossypium mexicanum). The white cotton adapts readily to machine spinning but the brown does not. Over the past century hand spinning has been gradually passing out of use and machine-spun yarns substituted, but this process is not yet entirely complete. The brown cotton, formerly used extensively in such towns as Tecpán, Chichicastenango, Comalapa, and San Juan Sacatepéquez is also gradually passing out of use, and yarns colored brown with dye are being used instead.

Of the natural dyes mentioned, indigo is the only one to have maintained any importance in the twentieth century. It is still used in dyeing yarns for skirt fabrics, although this is done on a commercial scale, not domestically. Cochineal, a tiny insect that feeds on the prickly pear cactus, was once the basis of an important dyeing industry in Guatemala, but O'Neale found only one workshop where it was still being used in 1936. Shellfish purple, a dye secreted by various species of molluscs when irritated, was not encountered by O'Neale at all. Yarns dyed with this substance are in fact extremely rare in existing Guatemalan textiles. However, in some pieces made before 1940, a commercial yarn imported from Honduras is found which has been dyed to imitate the somewhat uneven color of true shellfish purple (see Color Plates VIII and XVI). This may be easily recognized since it differs from Guatemalan handspun yarns in being made of three single yarns twisted together. Thus colors in most surviving Guatemalan textiles are derived from commercially produced chemical dyes. Some few other natural dyestuffs were recorded by O'Neale for dyeing wool, a fiber that is much easier to dye than is cotton. The commercial yarns available for Guatemalan weaving come from a variety of sources, both domestic and imported. In some areas, certain imported red yarns were highly prized, especially for skirts, and are now almost impossible to get.

Brocading yarns vary substantially both in color and texture. In turn-of-the-century textiles, cotton is the most common brocading thread, especially in red, yellow, yellow-orange, and green. Silk occurs rarely, usually in a beautiful dark pink color, perhaps

(continued page 41)

Color Plates

Plate No. I

Left: Nebaj belt collected by
Lilly de Jongh Osborne
(195), probably dating to the
Thirties. Cotton and silk.
8′5″x 3½″ (2.57 x .09 m.)
Right: Nebaj belt collected
1967-1975. Cotton. 8′4″ x
3⅜″ (2.54 x .085 m.).
American Museum of
Natural History 65/5910.

Plate No. II

Quezaltenango huipil collected by Lilly de
Jongh Osborne (2), probably dating before
1935. Cotton and silk. 38½ x 41½″ (98 x 105 cm.).

San Juan Sacatepéquez cofradía man's
shirt collected by Lilly de Jongh Osborne
(327) 1971. Cotton and silk. 20 x 21" (51 x 53 cm.).

Plate No. IV

Nahualá man's sash (detail) collected by
Lilly de Jongh Osborne (260). Cotton,
rayon, and silk. 8'2" x 11¾" (250 x 30 cm.).

Plate No. V

Nahualá man's tzute collected by Lilly de
Jongh Osborne (261) probably before
1960. Cotton. 27½ x 26″ (70 x 66 cm.).

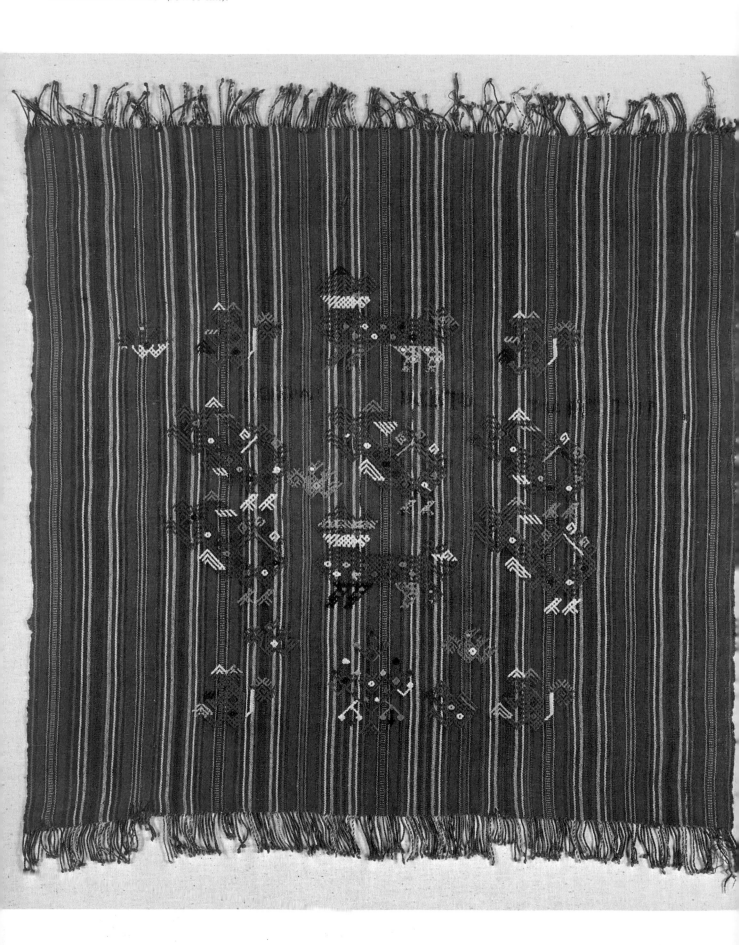

Plate No. VI

Chichicastenango woman's tzute collected by F. H. Lamson-Scribner in the late Thirties. Cotton. 32¾ x 34½" (83 x 87.5 cm.). Textile Museum 1964.65.34.

Plate No. VII

Todos Santos huipil collected by Lilly de Jongh Osborne (235), probably dating from the Sixties or early Seventies. Osborne's tag indicates it took six months to weave. Cotton and wool. 28¼ x 30" (72 x 76 cm.).

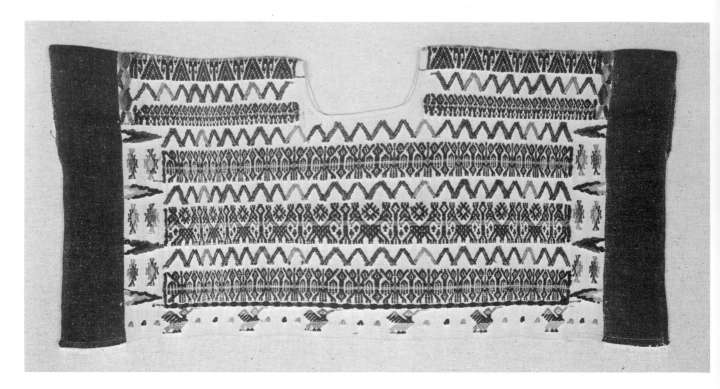

Plate No. VIII

Palín huipil collected by F. H. Lamson-Scribner in the late Thirties. Cotton. 13¾ x 28¼ " (35 x 71.5 cm.). 1964.65.12.

Plate No. IX

Totonicapán cofradía man's overpants collected by Lilly de Jongh Osborne (44c), probably dating c. 1900. Silk. 37¾ x 13¾" (96 x 35 cm.).

Plate No. X

Santiago Atitlán men's pants (detail), probably c. 1950. Cotton. 11½" (29 cm.) (width). Textile Museum 1965.66.11.

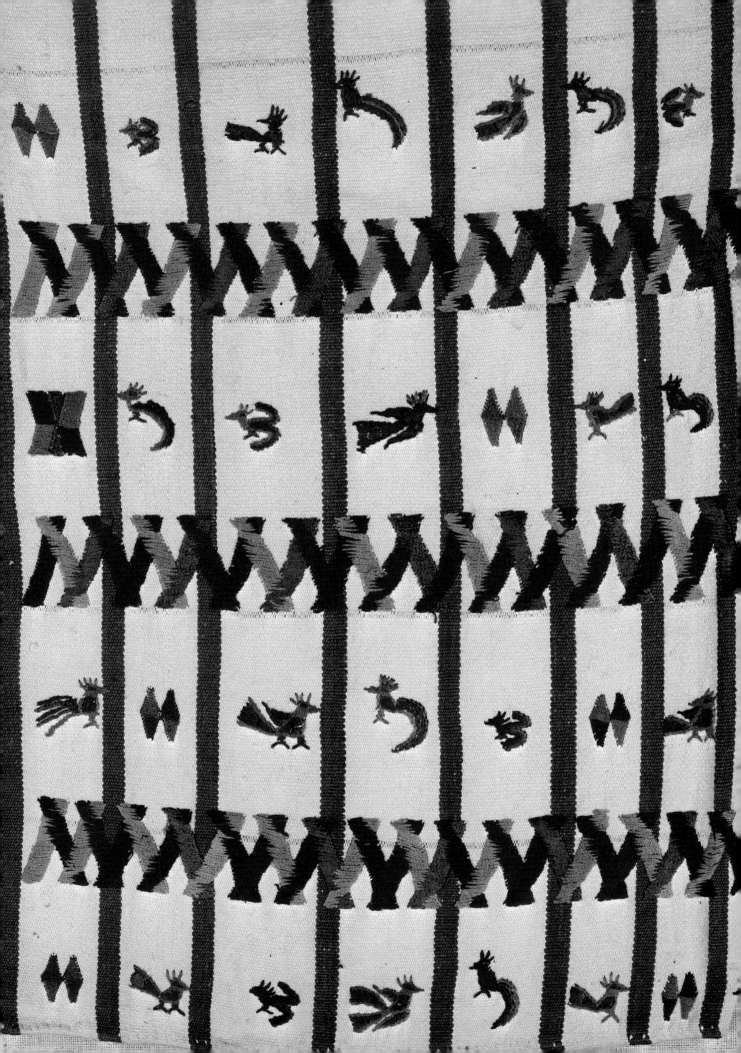

Plate No. XI

Nebaj huipil (detail), probably from the
Thirties. Cotton and silk. 28¾ x 44" (73 x
112 cm.) overall, 20½" (52 cm.) width of
center panel. Middle American Research
Institute, Tulane University G.4.4.7. Gift
of Mrs. Harold H. Stream.

Plate No. XII

San Martín Sacatepéquez huipil (detail of patterned area opened out flat) collected by Lilly de Jongh Osborne (309), probably dating from the Sixties. Cotton. 61 x 32¾″ (155 x 83 cm.).

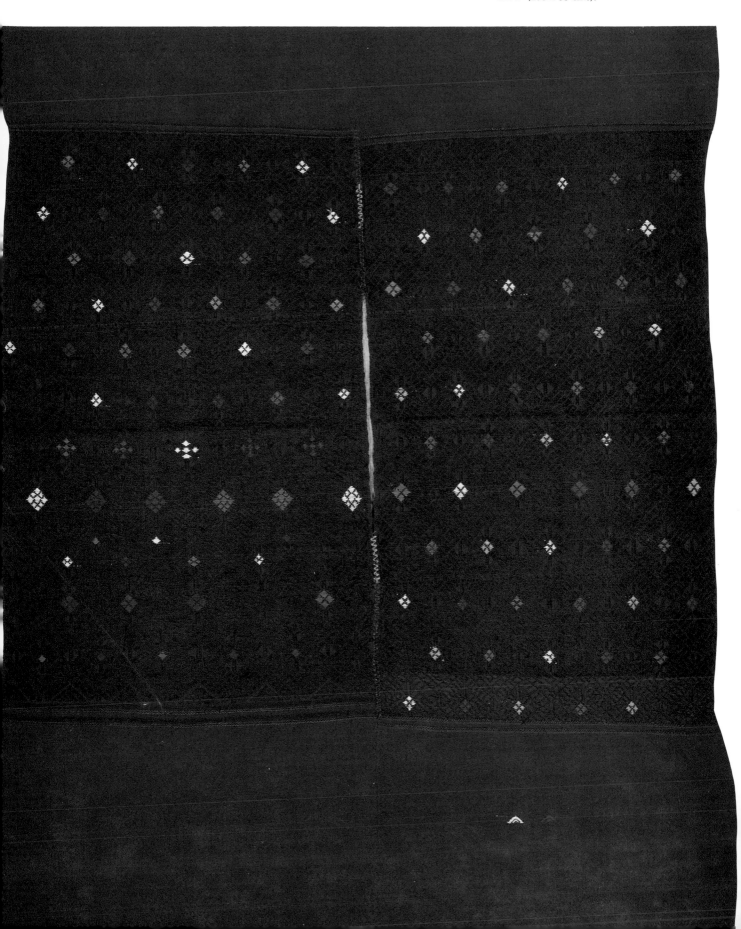

Plate No. XIII

San Mateo Ixtatán huipil, probably c.
1930. Cotton, wool, and silk. 33½ x 46″
(.85 x 1.19 m.). Middle American
Research Institute, Tulane University 41-423.

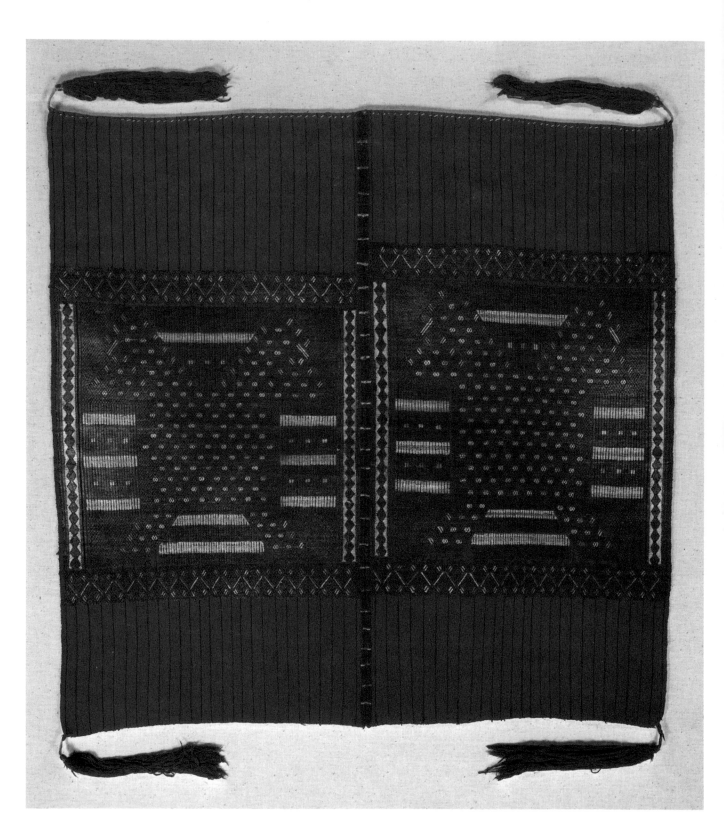

Plate No. XIV

Chichicastenango man's
tzute collected by F. H.
Lamson-Scribner in the late
Thirties. Cotton and silk.
30 x 30¾″ (76.5 x 78 cm.).
Textile Museum 1964.65.11.

Plate No. XV

San Martín Sacatepéquez
man's shirt, detail of sleeve,
collected in 1940. Cotton
and silk. 14½ x 8¼″ (37 x
21 cm.) (sleeve only). Textile
Museum 1965.51.49a.

Plate No. XVI

San Juan Sacatepéquez huipil collected by
Matilda Geddings Gray 1935. Cotton and
silk. 47¼ x 46½" (1.20 x 1.18 m.). Middle
American Research Institute, Tulane Uni-
versity 41.22A. Gift of Matilda Geddings
Gray (Tul 19 Wa).

from cochineal. In the 1930s silk was used much more lavishly, notably in beautiful textiles from Chichicastenango, Quezaltenango, Comalapa, and San Martín Jilotepeque. Various shades of purple, including magenta and deep purple, were especially common but aqua and yellow-orange are also found. Wool was also used for brocading from a comparatively early date in some towns such as Todos Santos. In the 1970s it was almost completely supplanted by acrylic, a man-made fiber of similarly fluffy texture which is marketed in very loud colors (such as hot pink and yellow-green) which do not fade, although the yarns do not resist wear well. Mercerized cottons have also been available since World War II. Mercerization is a chemical process which increases the sheen of the fiber. Such yarns come in a very broad range of colors, more brilliant than non-mercerized. It may be possible eventually to determine the period of use of many types of yarn fairly precisely, providing a method for dating undocumented specimens. Although this is a worthy project, it is beyond the scope of the present study.

Another general type of change to be noted is in the scale of the brocaded (or embroidered) design. In quite a few villages, textiles from early in the century have much smaller and fewer design motifs than do more recent examples. The brocaded huipils of San Juan Sacatepéquez and Todos Santos illustrate this change dramatically, as do the embroidered huipils of San Mateo Ixtatán and Santiago Atitlán. It is possible that the change is due to the easy availability of machine-spun yarns, which eliminate the need for long hours of spinning and so increase the amount of time available for weaving. Also the availability of brightly colored yarns may stimulate the weavers, whose love of color is widely known. In some instances, as in San Juan Sacatepéquez, the weaving standards have coarsened, but often the weaving is just as fine as ever (Todos Santos).

The most interesting changes, however, are those which are specific to individual towns. They include such things as a change from three-breadth to two-breadth huipils; changes in techniques of brocading; and new types of designs, sometimes internally devised, sometimes borrowed from other towns, and only occasionally borrowed from European sources. There are more of such changes than one would expect, given the overall first impression one gets that fewer and fewer people are wearing native dress. Far from being rigidly conservative culturally and incapable of innovation except in the adoption of European traits, Guatemalan weavers show a definite internal dynamic of change, subtle, perhaps, but important, and rewarding to appreciate.

It should be noted that no change is sudden, or uniformly adopted by everyone at once. Changes are usually gradual, occurring initially on a fraction of specimens and slowly increasing. Frequently, older women will continue to wear the style popular in their youth and people living farther away from town will dress more conservatively than those in town. The dates suggested in the following chapters for specific changes indicate only when an innovation first occurred and are not meant to imply that the older style ceased to be used at the same time. Both styles will occur simultaneously for a time until the older style dies out. This can take as long as fifty years, although not all do.

NOTES

1. This overview follows Handbook Vol. 7 1969 pp. 38-39.
2. See Colby and Berghe 1969 pp, 33-34, 71ff.
3. Most remarkable are the scraps of fabrics recovered from the cenote at Chichen Itza. See Mahler 1965. See Delgado 1968a for loom representations.
4. See Borhegyi 1965 p. 16.
5. Anawalt 1975 Part III pp. 349-367.
6. Anawalt 1975 pp. 364-365.
7. O'Neale 1945 p. 55 treadle loom speed; Sperlich 1980, p. 86 backstrap loom speed; O'Neale 1945 p. 53 cites a woman who could weave 6 wefts per minute, but this seems to have been unusual.
8. See Pang 1977a for a list of her publications.
9. See Sperlich 1980 pp. 2-5.
10. Sperlich 1980 p. 5.

CHAPTER TWO
Palín

Palín is located at an elevation of 3,695 feet (1,126m.), lower and farther south, and thus warmer, than most of the rest of the highland villages where weaving is still practiced, and this may be why its characteristic huipil is relatively small. Palín is also the only Pocomám Central village where weaving is still done. In 1948 it had a population of around 9,500.[1] The town is famous for its huge ancient ceiba tree under which the market is held.

The Palín huipil is a single piece of fabric, about 27″ (70 cm.) wide, white, with a broad red stripe along each side. Since the sides are seamed, the red stripe shows chiefly at the armholes when it is worn. A square hole is cut for the neck, and the edges are hemmed. It is about waist length and so is not worn tucked in. Usually there is a selvedge at only one end; the other end is hemmed. The central portion is decorated with supplementary-weft patterning. The sides and bottom of this area are decorated more sparsely than the center and shoulders. Everyday huipils usually have rows of horizontal zigzags, animals, and sometimes sideways chevron designs (see Figs. 1 and 3).[2] Huipils for more formal wear such as cofradía have geometric and bird motifs in more tightly and evenly spaced rows (Fig. 2). Some of these have a large double-headed bird in the upper part (Fig. 4), a design definitely associated with cofradía use.[3]

The technique used to weave the designs on the huipil in Figure 1, which appears to be the same as that used for the horizontal zigzags (and stepped diamonds) in the huipil in Color Plate VIII, is with the supplementary weft passed through an *open* plain-weave shed parallel to the ground weft. The distance travelled in one direction by the supplementary weft is short and the main color effect on the front is produced by the turn of the weft at the edges. A little extra length of thread is allowed to stand out from the edge in a loop to heighten this effect.

The dots that are so characteristic of Palín textiles, found scattered on the outer edges of the huipils, and covering the whole background of the tzutes (Figs. 8-10), are made with essentially the same technique. The only difference is that the brocading thread for the dots is inserted with the middle of the yarn put under one warp. Then the two ends are taken together and put under the two warps above the first in the next (open) shed. They are put under two or three warps above in the next shed and under two warps in the

fourth shed, after which the ends are usually cut off close to the fabric. In an alternative method of weaving dots, less common than the first, the middle of the yarn is again put under the one warp, but instead of being doubled to be carried back and forth in succeeding sheds, the two ends pass across each other in opposite directions. This type of dot is also complete in four sheds. It has a more symmetrical appearance than the first type of dot.

These techniques appear to be the only ones employed on the late nineteenth century everyday huipil in Fig. 1. For the principal designs on the type of huipil represented by Figs. 2 and 4, the supplementary weft is inserted on a *closed* plain-weave shed and floats on the front to create the designs and on the back between the design areas. The floats are over multiples of two warps, though their exact length is dependent on the particular motif. The lower edges of the design areas in these huipils are framed by a band of six wefts of the same kind used for the brocading, usually red and mauve. The two colors are woven alternately with floats of equal length on both faces (about ¼″, 6-7 mm.). The ends of these wefts are carried vertically along the side edges of the principal design area and are held in place by the supplementary wefts of the main design area turning around them.

Some huipils collected in the early Thirties match those in Gordon's photographs in having a similarly limited range of techniques and designs.[4] Other huipils from the Thirties contain, in addition, other kinds of designs woven with slightly different techniques. These new designs thus appear to have been introduced in the Thirties or not long before. They seem for the most part to have been borrowed from other villages.

The animal designs that appear around the edge of the huipil in Fig. 4 (and in the tzutes) are one such innovation. They are woven on a closed shed but have floats of regular length aligned in alternate pairs. This device occurs in the bodies of some of the larger birds on the cofradía huipil but is by no means a major component of those designs. The animals are similar in character to those found on textiles from several Cakchiquel villages, although San Pedro Sacatepéquez is the most likely source, since it has been making textiles for sale to other villages for a long time.

Another motif probably borrowed from a foreign town is the sideways chevrons or vertical

Fig.1 Palín woman, late nineteenth century. Peabody Museum,
Harvard University. Photograph by George Byron Gordon.

zigzag motif. These are found on the edges of huipils, such as the one in Color Plate VIII, or across the main design area of some everyday huipils, and on sashes. They are woven with the supplementary weft floating on the front, held down at intervals by single warps. The floats are in alternate alignment and the "tie-down" warps are unobtrusive. Such designs are common on some San Pedro Sacatepéquez huipils as well as on those from San Martín Jilotepeque, another town that was producing huipils for sale at the turn of the century.[5]

A third new design is the row of diamonds next to the red band over the shoulder found on most twentieth-century huipils from the late Thirties on (See Fig. 4 and Color Plate VIII). To form the diamonds, the supplementary weft floats on the front of the fabric and is held down by only a single warp at the edges. The turn of the weft on the front makes a ridge on the edge of the design similar to that formed for the horizontal zigzag designs. There is no obvious outside source for this design and it may have been a local innovation.

The most obvious differences between huipils of the Thirties and more recent huipils seem to depend more on the types of yarns used than on the technique and design considerations outlined above which distinguish pre-1930 from post 1930 examples. Huipils from the Thirties, such as the example in Color Plate VIII, are often woven of unbleached handspun cotton yarns, which gives the textile a crepy quality not found in newer pieces woven of machine-spun yarns. The brocading yarns of these older huipils are often either the imitation-shellfish purple yarn (Fig. 4, and to some extent in Color Plate VIII) or a yarn consisting of red and blue singles plied together (see Color Plate VIII). The latter is somewhat more common. The red and blue plied yarns seem to have continued in use through the Forties,[6] but it is not clear when after that they passed out of use. Since at least 1965 Palín textiles have been brocaded with shiny mercerized cotton yarns in a variety of colors, though mauve and red still predominate.

Plain white huipils are also sometimes worn in Palín for everyday activities as in many towns. These are made the same size and shape as the decorated huipils, but are of machine-made fabric. Five or six narrow vertical tucks may be made on each side of the neck hole with a sewing machine.[7]

Skirts appear to have been made and worn in relatively consistent fashion from the Thirties to the present.[8] The skirt is made of two lengths of dark blue, treadle-loom woven fabric, each about 23" (59 cm.) wide and 6½′ (2 m.) long, which have been sewn side to side, after which the ends are joined to form a tube

Fig. 2 Palín woman in ceremonial huipil and hair style, late nineteenth century. Peabody Museum, Harvard University. Photograph by George Byron Gordon.

Fig. 3 Palín woman, 1935. Middle American Research Institute, Tulane University, Matilda Geddings Gray Collection.

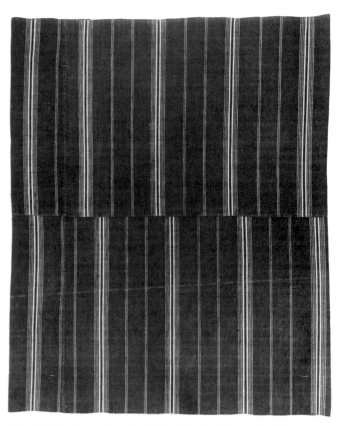

Fig. 5 Palín skirt collected by Lilly de Jongh Osborne (98). Cotton. 45¾ x 37¾″ (116 x 96 cm.).

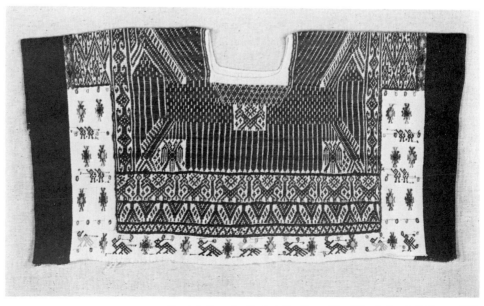

Fig. 4 Palín cofradía huipil collected by Lilly de Jongh Osborne (91), probably dating before 1940. Cotton. 14½ x 28¼″ (37 x 72 cm.).

(Fig. 5). This skirt is relatively narrow in comparison with that of many other towns. The seaming is usually done by machine so it is not visible except for the disjunction of the striping, worn at the hipline just below the belt. The most characteristic striping (Fig. 3) is with pairs of fine white weft stripes at about 2" (5-6 cm.) intervals, which are worn vertical. An alternative skirt design (Fig. 5) is similar, but every third pair of stripes is wider and is surrounded by three additional pairs of narrow stripes. To wear the skirt, the woman steps into the tube, folds down the extra length at the top, and forms three large pleats in the back which are secured by the sash (Fig. 3). Mid-calf length, as in Fig. 3, is customary, although it may be worn longer (Fig. 1).

The sash (Fig. 6) is red, usually with a few narrow dark blue or black warp stripes. It appears that older examples may be wider than newer ones. The one seen in Fig. 1 appears to be at least a foot wide, and examples collected in the Thirties range from 9 to 14" (23-36 cm.), while modern examples such as the one in Fig. 6 vary between 6 and 8" (15-20 cm.).[9] The example in Fig. 6 is warp-faced with much thicker wefts than warps, giving it a ribbed appearance. The older, wider sashes have finer wefts and so are more flexible. The belt in Fig. 1 is very sparsely patterned and only horizontal zigzags are visible. One row of zigzags appears to be brocaded in the same way as the huipils and the other appears similar to those on modern belts, in which the supplementary weft is inserted in an open shed and wrapped around the raised warps. The lack of horizontal chevrons on this belt correlates with the design repertoire of the huipil. In modern belts both ends are brocaded for about 30" (76 cm.), one end having horizontal zigzags and horizontal chevrons and the other end with bands of vertical zigzags. The horizontal chevrons and vertical zigzags (clearly related motifs) are brocaded in the same manner as in huipils and were probably introduced at the same time into both sashes and huipils. Sashes from the Thirties are often brocaded in silk, whereas recent examples are brocaded in cotton. A variety of different colors are used. Sashes from the Thirties are fringed. In Fig. 6 and other recent pieces, heading strips are woven on the ends of the sash, but the warps are left unwoven for 6-7" (15-18 cm.) between the main woven area and the heading. The warps are cut about an inch (2-3 cm.) beyond the heading. The sash is worn with the ends tucked in over the pleats (Fig. 3) and the decoration is usually visible on the front.

The everyday hairdress is not especially remarkable; hair is usually simply bound to the head (see Figs. 1 and 3). However, for ceremonial wear, an elegant hairstyle employing a long handwoven ribbon

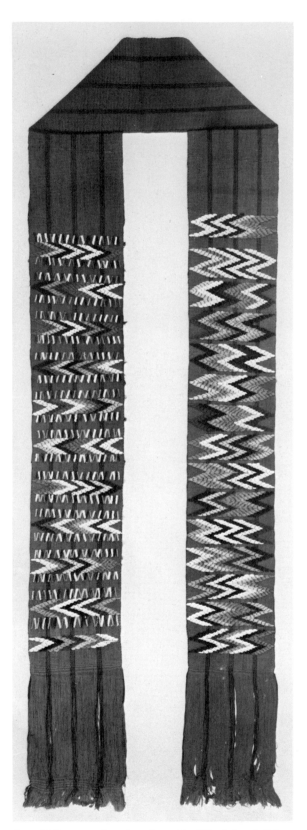

Fig. 6 Palín woman's sash, collected by Lilly de Jongh Osborne (277), probably dating after 1960. Cotton. 8½' x 6" (260 x 15.5 cm.).

has been used (Figs. 2, 7). The example from the Osborne collection (Fig. 7) is obviously exactly the same as the one shown in Gordon's photograph (Fig. 2).[10] It is made of heavy purplish red wool yarns alternating with fine white cotton warps and with cotton wefts. It has a narrow border of blue cotton warps along each side.[11] The weft is similar to the white cotton warps but is used tripled. The weave is warp-faced alternating float weave.[12] That is, alternate warps (wool) interlace 3/1 and the 3-span floats are in alternating alignment. The white warps interlace 1/1. The heavy wool warp floats cover the front of the band, and corresponding weft floats appear on the back (Fig. 8). Since the band is warp-faced, the warp floats appear to be much longer than the weft floats. The band in Fig. 8 is 70½' (21.50 m.) in length, of which 53½' (16.30 m.) is in one continuous piece and the rest is of shorter lengths stitched together. The splicing was probably necessitated by its generally worn condition. This ribbon is wrapped spirally around two locks of hair. The hair locks may simply cross over each other at the crown of the head, or they may be knotted together in such a way as to form an upright projection over the forehead.[13] When not being worn, the band is kept wound into a ball.[14]

Tzutes are usually about a yard square (1 m.) and, like the huipils, are usually hemmed at one end. They have a white ground and red borders on all four sides, an unusual arrangement in Guatemalan textiles. Because the weaving is warp-predominant, however, the warpwise borders show more clearly than the weftwise ones. The border may consist of a pair of narrow lines with small brocaded motifs in between (Fig. 9), or of one or more broad unbrocaded bands (Figs. 8 and 10). Older tzutes have one or two bands; some more recent ones have three (Fig. 10). Both types have an inner border of geometric pattern, a simple zigzag or diamond in most older pieces (Fig. 8 and 9), although more elaborate ones are found on some pieces after about 1960 (Fig. 10). The central portion of tzutes from the early Thirties and before are brocaded only with dots and the same kind of stepped diamond design that occurs on the edges of older huipils.[15] The central portion of tzutes from the Thirties and later is usually decorated with small brocaded animals against a ground filled with dots. The dots may be more closely spaced on newer pieces than on older ones, although the tzute in Fig. 8, which was collected in the late Thirties, has a generous number. As with huipils, the type of yarns used for the ground and supplementary wefts are also related to date of manufacture. Some tzutes after 1960 have orange stripes rather than red ones. The tzute is draped over one shoulder when not being used.

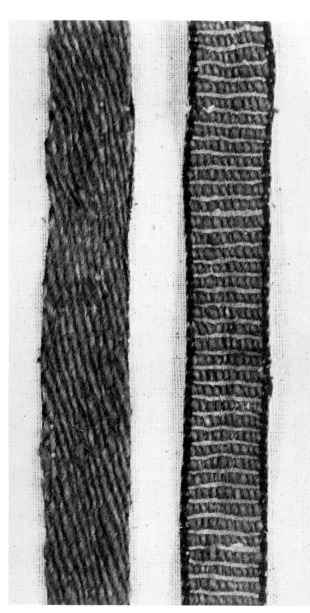

Fig. 7 Palín hair ribbon, details of front and back, collected by Lilly de Jongh Osborne (88), dated 1912 by her. Wool and cotton. Width: 1" (2.5 cm.).

Fig. 8 Palín tzute, collected by F.H. Lamson-Scribner in the late Thirties. Cotton. 27½ x 28¾" (70 x 73 cm.). Textile Museum 1964.65.81.

Fig. 9 Palín tzute, collected by Lilly de Jongh Osborne (95h), probably dating after 1950. Cotton. 30¼ x 28½" (77 x 72 cm.).

Fig. 10 Palín tzute, collected by Lilly de Jongh Osborne (95d), probably dating after 1960. Cotton. 34¼ x 32" (87 x 81 cm.) (maxima).

Fig. 11 Palín servilleta, collected by Lilly de Jongh Osborne (136), probably dating before 1960. Cotton. 31½ x 30" (80 x 76 cm.).

Servilletas, distinguished from tzutes by fringed ends and broad weft striping, appear much more seldom in collections than tzutes (Fig. 11). Older examples such as the one illustrated, which may be dated by its use of blue and red plied yarns, have weft stripes in red and blue (against white) alternating with bands of zigzags brocaded in the more conservative techniques. Some examples, such as the one in Fig. 11, also have three vertical red stripes, one on each side and one down the center.[16] The warp ends are knotted for the fringe, and small colored tassels are added. An example from 1970 in the Textile Musem collection has all red stripes (including three warp stripes) and elaborate brocaded motifs similar to those in the borders of newer tzutes such as Fig. 10.[17] The fringe lacks tassels.

NOTES

1. This figure, and those given for the other towns covered, is based on information in Kelsey and Osborne, Revised Edition. It includes the entire municipio, in other words, not only the town itself, but also the surrounding countryside where the costume is also worn.
2. See also Muñoz and Ward 1940, p. 171, pl. 38, and Osborne 1965, pl. 21b (1975, p. 149).
3. See also Marden 1947, p. 560, a scene with seven women at a ceremonial meal. Four of the women clearly have on huipils with a large double-headed bird. One has a huipil of the type shown in Fig. 2, one has an everyday huipil, and the other is not clearly visible. Four of the huipils (either with the large double-headed bird or not visible) have broad pink ribbons attached at the neckline, a common addition for specifically cofradía huipils (see also the section on Nahualá).
4. For example, Peabody Museum 41-90/14259, collected in 1934, which resembles the huipil in Fig. 2, and 32-37/114, collected in 1932, which is similar but has a large double-headed bird.
5. See O'Neale 1945, Fig. 85b (labelled Mixco but probably not woven there) and Fig. 68l for San Pedro examples; Fig. 86 for San Martín examples.
6. See Marden 1947, p. 560.
7. An example of this type of huipil was collected for the Textile Museum in 1970 and was photographed in use by Marion Stirling Pugh. In the Matilda Gray collection at Tulane there are photographs of Palín women in plain white huipils from the Thirties. See also Kelsey and Osborne 1939/61 4th plate after p. 56 (right).
8. Includes (besides Figs. 3, 5) all the photographs cited in the list of references as well as two skirts in the Textile Museum collection (collected 1970) and a photograph by Marion Stirling Pugh. The skirt in the Palmer collection described by O'Neale (1945, p. 285, Figs. 42h, 52x) is so different in every way from all the others that it seems to be a case of erroneous attribution.
9. O'Neale (1945, p. 285) says the example in the Gray collection is 14″ wide and the Palmer one is 9″. Two Textile Museum sashes similar to Fig. 6 collected in 1970 are 18.5 and 21.5 cm. wide (1970.21.15 and 1970.21.20).
10. The example in Fig. 7 does not exactly match O'Neale's description, p. 70 or diagram, Fig. 23s, of a specimen from the Palmer collection (which is evidently identical to a band from Santa María de Jesús in the Gray collection).
11. The exact warp count is 1 white cotton warp, 5 blue cotton warps, 24 red wool alternating with 22 white cotton warps, 5 blue cotton warps, and 1 white cotton warp.
12. See Emery 1966, pp. 113-15 for a discussion of this terminology.
13. In the Marden photograph cited above in Note 2 (1947, p. 560) four of the women wear the hair locks simply crossed and three

wear it with the forehead projections.
14. Nobuko Kajitani, personal communication. She visited Palín in 1973.
15. For example, Peabody Museum 32-37/115 and 117, collected in 1932; 970-24/23730, also collected in the Thirties; and Textile Museum 1964.65.92, collected in the late Thirties.
16. The Osborne collection also inclues a servilleta without warp stripes. A similar piece is described by O'Neale 1945, p. 285.
17. 1970.21.13. Gift of Marion Stirling Pugh.

REFERENCES
Ethnographic photographs:
Kelsey and Osborne 1939/61, 4th plate after p.56, woman
Muñoz and Ward 1940, pl. 38, p. 171, standing woman (pl. 5 p. 42, market)
Lemos 1941, p. 7 top left, market
Marden 1947, p. 560, color, seated women, cofradía
Osborne 1965, pl. 21b, standing woman (1975 p. 149)
Bjerregaard 1977, pl. 21, color, seated woman
Textiles:
Lemos 1941, p. 25 no. 3 (color) tzute
O'Neale 1945, fig. 115a (LMO coll.) small tzute for candles
Atwater 1965 ed., pl. IIIa, huipil with large double-headed bird
                  pl. IIId, belt (detail)
                  pl. IVa, tzute with aberrant pictorial design
                  pl. IVb, small tzute for candles
Osborne 1965, pl. 14a tzute with diamond borders (1975 p. 92)
Sowards 1974, p.5, huipil (TM 1964.65.5 coll. 1937-40)
Bjerregaard, 1977, p. 52, huipil with large double-headed bird
Heard Museum 1979, p. 83 bottom, no. 21, color, woman's costume
Color Renderings:
Crocker 1952, pl. 10
Osborne 1965, pl. 82 right, black and white (1975 p. 267)
Wood and Osborne 1966, pl. 14
Petterson 1977, no. 31, p. 158-9
Drawings:
O'Neale 1945, Fig. 24m huipil design layout, Fig. 71g, 72e and f designs
Atwater 1946, p. 33, diagram 17, huipil
             p. 39, diagram 22, tzute
Start 1948, fig. 16, p. 43-44, tzute
Text:
O'Neale 1945, pp. 284-5
Delgado 1963, p. 286, museum specimens

CHAPTER THREE
San Juan Sacatepéquez

San Juan Sacatepéquez is close enough to Guatemala City that its women are seen there in the Central Market selling flowers and vegetables. It is a large village of nearly 30,000 in 1948 and has a particularly large and diverse textile repertory. It is one of several Cakchiquel villages in the area that have relatively fancy hand weaving.

Describing the San Juan Sacatepéquez huipil is complicated by the fact that several different types have been woven simultaneously. The everyday huipils have a basic format in common, however. They are composed of two pieces of fabric sewn together with a randa. A round hole is cut for the neck. The hole is usually overcast with buttonhole stitches. Often a few inches of the front seam are left open below the neck and also overcast, with little tie cords at the top. The sides are not sewn together, although this is not readily apparent as it is worn, since the ends are tucked into the skirt and belt. The huipil is so wide that it falls down to the elbows as normally worn (see Fig. 12).[1] The decoration on all San Juan textiles is woven on a closed plain-weave shed, with the supplementary wefts floating across design areas on the front and floating between them on the back.

At least three types of everyday huipils seem to have been current in the Thirties.[2] One is white with ½" mauve warp stripes at about 3" intervals (Fig. 13). It has a band of supplementary-weft patterning in red and mauve across the shoulder line, usually animals framed with horizontal zigzags. This seems to be the type of huipil represented in the late nineteenth century photograph (Fig. 12) and may have been the most popular style before the Thirties.[3] Another style of huipil has a solid dark blue ground (Fig. 14). It has a similar band of supplementary-weft patterning on the shoulder and rows of additional motifs below. The most frequently illustrated and collected huipil, however, is the one represented by Color Plate XVI. It has warp stripes in the improbable but unmistakable combination of red, yellow, mauve, and natural brown cotton. Some examples have no supplementary-weft patterning, while others have a band across the shoulders, usually consisting of two rows of animals framed by horizontal zigzags, predominantly in yellow silk and mauve cotton. The mauve in this case is the imitation shellfish-dyed yarn.

The few available illustrations of huipils from the Forties show examples of the red-yellow-mauve-brown striped and dark blue types with shoulder bands of supplementary-weft patterning that are broader than before, the greater breadth achieved by increasing the scale of the individual designs.[4] In the Fifties, in addition to the solid navy blue huipils, examples with solid red, dark green or white grounds occur and there is a white ground huipil with brown, red, purple, green, and gold stripes.[5] The red, mauve, yellow, and brown huipil is still the most common, however. Apparently some three-breadth huipils also occur.[6]

Today, the white ground with stripes and the solid color huipils are scarcely seen, although some green ground examples apparently were made in the Sixties.[7] The red-yellow-mauve-brown striped huipil has become predominantly yellow and mauve rather than predominantly red. The scale of the designs has continued to increase and another row of animals has been added on each side (see Fig. 16). Brocading is usually done with heavy mercerized cotton thread in yellow, blue, green, and purple, plus other colors in small amounts. The size of the designs and the thickness of the brocading threads gives an effect of greater coarseness than is the case with older huipils, although the actual thread count of the ground fabric may not differ greatly in the better examples. The weft counts may be lower in some examples however; there may be 15 wefts per inch (6 per cm.) rather than 20 (8 per cm.).

The modern manner of wearing the huipil may also differ, although some women still wear it in the traditional way. The two women in the foreground of Fig. 15 have the outside edges of the huipil folded under so that it only covers the shoulders. A commercial blouse is worn underneath.

The cofradía huipil of the Thirties is illustrated in Figs. 17 and 18. It is of three pieces, with white ground, and is sewn together with purple and red randas. Unlike the everyday huipil, the side seams are sewn, perhaps because it is not worn tucked in (see Fig. 17). It has a round neck hole the edges of which are bound with blue taffeta ribbon and with blue taffeta roundels front and back. The fabric has horizontal ribs made by using heavier wefts. The shoulder area of the side panels and most of the central panel have supplementary-weft patterning in mauve and red cotton forming animal designs. The zones of motifs in the

Fig. 12 San Juan Sacatepéquez woman, late nineteenth century.
Peabody Museum, Harvard University. Photograph by George
Byron Gordon.

central panel are separated by red weft stripes. This style of cofradía huipil continued in use at least through the late Fifties.[8]

Another type of ceremonial huipil is also found. Examples from the Thirties are more rare than the preceding type.[9] Recent examples also occur (Fig. 19). This huipil is also of three pieces, has weft ribbing, blue taffeta on the neckline and roundels, and is sewn up the sides. The side seams are sewn with the same type of randa as is used for the other seaming, which was not the case with the huipils in Figs. 17 and 18. The fabric is white with broad purple warp stripes, and only the shoulder line has supplementary weft patterning, in red and purple. The purple stripes are slightly wider in Fig. 19 than in examples from the Thirties and the scale of the supplementary weft patterning is also slightly larger.

The most characteristic skirt (Fig. 20) is made of two lengths of blue cotton treadle-loom woven fabric, joined side to side and at the ends to form a tube by randas, usually of predominantly purple silk or

Fig. 13 San Juan Sacatepéquez huipil, collected by Howard H. Tewksbury in the late Thirties. Cotton. 44½ x 47½" (113 x 121 cm.). Peabody Museum, Harvard University 970-24/23774. Gift of Howard H. Tewksbury. Photograph by Hillel Burger.

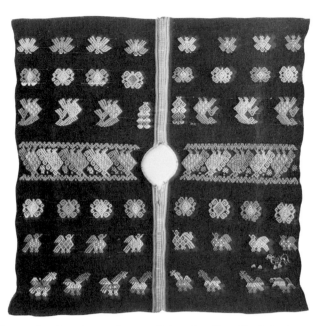

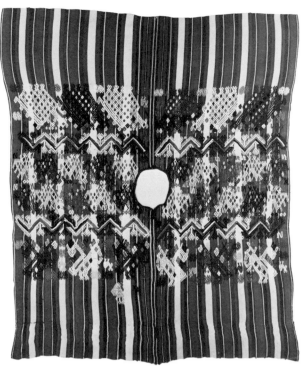

Fig. 14 San Juan Sacatepéquez girl's huipil, collected by Lilly de Jongh Osborne (62), probably from the Forties. Cotton. 34 x 34¾" (86 x 88 cm.).

Fig. 16 San Juan Sacatepéquez huipil, collected by Ambassador William G. Bowdler in 1972. Cotton. 53 x 43" (1.35 x 1.09 m.).

Fig. 15 San Juan Sacatepéquez women, 1975. Photograph by Marilyn Anderson; black and white from color original.

cotton thread. The fabric has white or very light blue warp and weft stripes, each two threads wide. A single such stripe alternates regularly with a cluster of three stripes in both directions. The warp stripes are closer together than the weft stripes, ½" (1.3 cm.) as against 1½" (3.5 cm.) so that rectangles are formed which are horizontal as the skirt is worn. The loom width of the fabric is 23" (59 cm.), the same as for the Palín skirts, but the length used is half again as much, each piece being 113" (2.86 m.) in the example shown in Fig. 20. The randa seems to have become wider since the beginning of the century as can be seen by comparing Figs. 12 and 20. The increase seems to have occurred in the late Thirties or early Forties.[10] The later randas may be as wide as 1⅝" (4 cm.). The stitch makes a simple over-and-under motion between the two fabrics, which are placed edge to edge. Usually two shades of purple alternate, with two or three stitches each, and with other colors inserted at about ¾" (2 cm.) intervals.

The skirt is worn wrapped snugly without pleats. Usually, although not invariably, the end falls on the left side coming from the back, with the vertical randa visible from the back and the horizontal randa at the hip. As at Palín, the extra length is folded down inside at the top. It is worn to just above ankle length, although younger women tend to wear their skirts slightly shorter.[11] Skirts made of double ikat fabric from Salcajá are also now worn by some women in the village (see Fig. 15, left).

The skirt is held in place either with a black and white striped wool belt or, more commonly, with a sash in the red, yellow, and mauve striping characteristic of the village (Fig. 20). The black and white belt is usually embroidered with small animal designs, and is similar to the embroidered belt of nearby San Pedro Sacatepéquez.[12] The black and white belts are not woven in the village and seem to be an intrusive form. The sashes, on the other hand, are of local style and manufacture. Although the striped sash is most common, solid color sashes also occur, in red, yellow, or dark blue.[13] All are patterned with rows of geometric or animal designs in a manner similar to the huipil. The ends have a long, often corded, fringe. Newer sashes are more coarsely woven than old ones and have cotton supplementary-weft patterning rather than the silk often found on older examples. The sash is worn spread out relatively flat, with the ends tucked under.

In the Thirties there were at least two ways of wearing the hair, one simply braided and wound around the head as seen in Fig. 12, and one with purple wool cords incorporated into the braids. In the latter style, the ends of the cords hang down behind the

ears.[14] The woman dressed for cofradía in Fig. 17 wears a Totonicapán ribbon, done into a knot over her forehead. The style with simple braids wound around the head is still common, though braids may also hang down the back (Fig. 15). Black wool cords are sometimes braided into the hair.[15]

There seem to be at least two types of women's tzutes, although information on this subject is scanty. Both are comparatively large, between three and four feet on a side, and made of two loom widths, often joined with a randa. One type is striped in red, yellow, mauve, and brown, in a manner much like that of the huipil. They may be plain, or brocaded with rows of animals.[16] This kind is generally used as a shawl, folded into a triangle, draped under the left arm and knotted on the right shoulder. Similarly slung it may also be used to carry things.[17] It may also be used as a head-cloth.[18] The second type has some dark blue stripes in addition to the red, yellow, mauve, and brown ones, and has narrower stripes in the center than at the sides, as in Fig. 21. It may be plain or have animals brocaded in informal arrangement in the corners (Fig. 21).[19] This type is generally used to cover goods carried in a basket on the head.[20]

A number of Cakchiquel towns make hand-woven caps for babies to wear to protect them from the sun and from strangers' eyes. Such a cap from San Juan Sacatepéquez is shown in Fig. 22. It is made from a small, four-selvedge rectangle 20" (51 cm.) x 7½" (19 cm.). The ends are overlapped and one side is gathered into a peak. This example is in natural brown cotton with mauve borders, brocaded with typical San Juan designs. Others are striped or dark blue. Some have bands of gauze weave as well as brocading.[21]

The man's everyday costume is now completely Europeanized, but before World War II some elements of native dress remained (Fig. 23). A sash, often striped like the woman's or solid color, as in Fig. 25, was worn with white pants. In addition, a jacket made in European cut but of backstrap-loom-woven fabric was used (Fig. 24). The fabric is red with fine brown stripes and occasional yellow or mauve stripes. The example illustrated separately seems to be finer than the one being worn, in Fig. 23, since it has black wool fabric collar and cuffs, black wool braid trim, and some supplementary-weft patterning along the lower edge. The jacket worn by the man on the right in the late nineteenth century photograph (Fig. 26) is also of this type.

The man's cofradía costume, still worn, is of greater interest. The seated man (at left) in the late ninteenth-century photograph (Fig. 26) wears essentially the same costume as is shown in Fig. 27 from the Thirties. The black wool pants are of European in-

Fig. 17 San Juan Sacatepéquez woman in cofradía costume, 1935.
Middle American Research Institute, Tulane University, Matilda
Geddings Gray Collection.

Fig. 18 San Juan Sacatepéquez cofradía huipil, collected by Matilda
Geddings Gray in 1935. Cotton with silk appliqué. 21¾ x 45¾" (.55
x 1.16 m.). Middle American Research Institute, Tulane University,
41.33A. Gift of Matilda Geddings Gray (Tul 28 Wa).

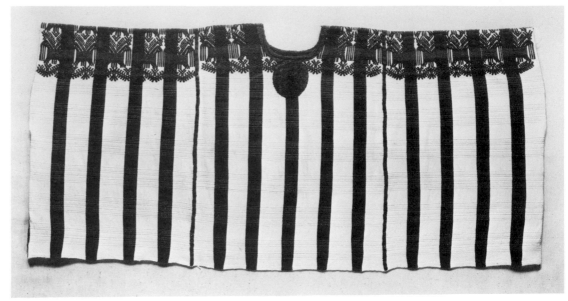

Fig. 19 San Juan Sacatepéquez cofradía huipil, collected by Ambassador William G. Bowdler in 1973. Cotton with silk appliqué. 23 x 48″ (.58 x 1.22 m.).

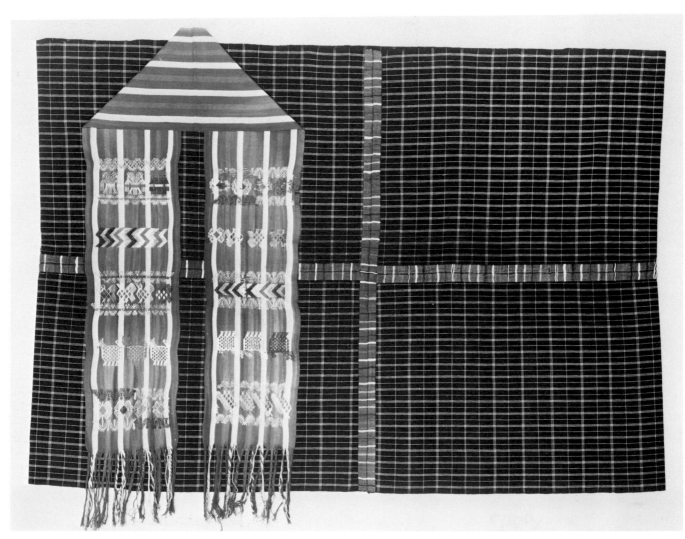

Fig. 20 San Juan Sacatepéquez skirt, collected by Ambassador William G. Bowdler in 1972. Cotton. 46 x 67¾″ (1.17 x 1.72 m.). Sash collected by Lilly de Jongh Osborne (65), probably dating from the Thirties. Cotton and silk. 7′4″ x 9¾″ (2.24 x .25 m.).

Fig. 21 San Juan Sacatepéquez woman's tzute collected by F.H. Lamson-Scribner in the late Thirties. Cotton and silk. 43¼ x 45¾" (1.10 x 1.16 m.). Textile Museum 1964.65.111.

Fig. 22 San Juan Sacatepéquez baby's cap collected by Lilly de Jongh Osborne (60). Cotton and silk. 8 x 7½" (20 x 19 cm.).

Fig. 23 San Juan Sacatepéquez man, 1935. Middle American Research Institute, Tulane University, Matilda Geddings Gray Collection.

Fig. 24 San Juan Sacatepéquez man's jacket, probably from the Thirties. Cotton, wool, and silk. 25½ x 18½″ (65 x 47 cm.) (width at bottom). Collection of Fifi White.

spiration but in an archaic cut and split partway up the leg. The shirt (color plate III) is woven on the backstrap loom. It is primarily of brown cotton, with fine white stripes. On the ends of the sleeves and on the bottom of the side panels are some colored stripes and a little zigzag brocading. At the shoulder is a roll of fabric which resembles that found on jackets or doublets worn by European men in the late sixteenth and early seventeenth century. Whether the connection was direct or through a Spanish rural intermediary link is uncertain.

In addition the man wears two large tzutes, similar in construction, one tied over his head and one draped over his shoulders. Both are large rectangles made of two loom panels. They are predominantly red, with some yellow and mauve warp stripes, and

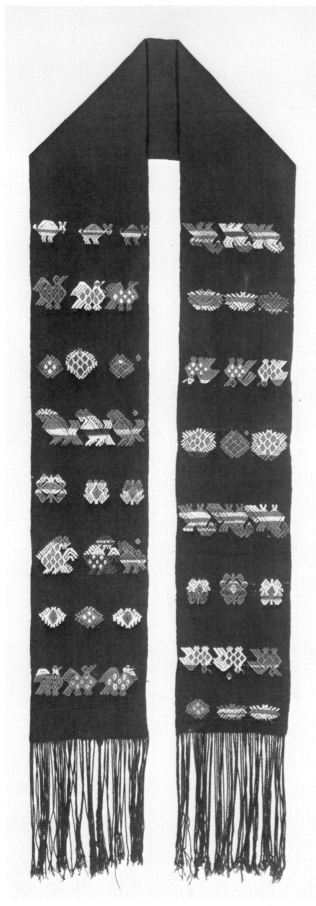

have a brocaded rectangular area in each corner. The shoulder tzute differs only in that it lacks the central brocaded area of the head tzute (Fig. 28 shows the head tzute). Each is folded into a triangle before being put on. The example shown in Fig. 28 may date from the Twenties since it has relatively small animals brocaded in silk, and the yellow and mauve stripes are relatively narrow. The gradually increasing width of the contrasting stripes can be seen by comparing the tzutes in Figs. 26 and 27. Modern tzutes have still broader stripes, as well as larger designs.

The small tzute in Fig. 29 is similar in design to the large ones just discussed. It is probably a later piece than the one in Fig. 28 since the contrast stripes are wider and the brocading is entirely in cotton. Mrs. Osborne's tag for this tzute says that it is used to put under the plate which receives the alms.

The panel shown in Fig. 30 is meant to hang from the front of the stand on which the statue of the saint rests.[22] This example is woven on a dark green ground. Others have a dark blue or yellow ground.[23] Pink (or yellow) wool braided tape is put around the outer edges. The lettering is embroidered in chain stitch, but the rest of the decoration is brocaded in the typical San Juan designs in red and mauve. The cross indicates the ecclesiastical function of the piece.

NOTES

1. In an interesting variation, the woman on the right in Start 1948 pl. IIa has tied up the width of her huipil with a cord around her neck.
2. O'Neale 1945, p. 269; Wood and Osborne 1966, pls. 2-4.
3. Popenoe 1924, p. 220, mentions only this style, although his description is very imprecise. Lothrop 1928b, lists this type first and describes it in most detail. It is also shown in Lee 1926, p. 609, woman at right.
4. See Marden 1947, especially p. 551 right.
5. Delgado 1963, p. 291. Similar striped huipils occur occasionally in the Thirties; they have wider stripes at the sides than in the center (Peabody Museum 32-37/147 and 970-24/23776).
6. Delgado 1963, p. 291; Crocker 1952, caption to pl. 9.
7. Example published by Marks 1973, p. 8 left. Another example is in the Jamison collection.
8. Delgado 1963, p. 293.
9. An example collected in the late Thirties and having false shellfish purple yarns is in the Peabody Museum (970-24/23772).
10. The skirts in Marden 1947, p. 551 right and 557 right, have wide randas. The older woman on p. 557 right has a skirt with a narrower randa than the younger woman. Earlier photographs such as Carnegie 1935 p. 158, Marden 1936 pl. III right, and Lemos 1941 p. 6 lower right, show skirts with narrow randas.
11. Pancake 1976, p. 7. This statement is confirmed by the photograph in Carnegie 1935, p. 158.
12. Illustration in Osborne 1935, pl. II, no. 11.
13. Dark blue sash: O'Neale 1945, fig. 122a; red sash: University Museum, Philadelphia, Osborne collection 42-35-207 labelled "ceremonial"; yellow sash: University Museum, Philadelphia, Tewksbury collection 66-34-16. Pancake 1976, p. 19, distinguishes between a maiden's sash and a matron's sash.
14. Illustrated in Marden 1947, pp. 540, 551 right. The woman on the left on p. 540 is probably from San Juan, although, as stated in the caption, the huipil she is wearing as a shawl is from San Pedro.

Fig. 25 San Juan Sacatepéquez man's sash collected by Lilly de Jongh Osborne (59), probably dating from the Thirties. Cotton and silk. 79 x 8¾″ (2.1 x .22 m.).

Fig. 26 San Juan Sacatepéquez men, late nineteenth century. Peabody Museum, Harvard University. Photograph by George Byron Gordon.

Fig. 27 San Juan Sacatepéquez man in cofradía costume, 1935: a, front; b, back. Middle American Research Institute, Tulane University, Matilda Geddings Gray Collection.

Fig. 28 San Juan Sacatepéquez cofradía tzute collected by Lilly de Jongh Osborne (57), probably dating from the Twenties. Cotton and silk. 52¾ x 43¾″ (1.34 x 1.11 m.).

Fig. 29 San Juan Sacatepéquez cofradía tzute collected by Lilly de Jongh Osborne (58), probably dating from the Forties or Fifties. Cotton. 23¼ x 22" (59 x 56 cm.).

Fig. 30 San Juan Sacatepéquez cofradía panel, probably dating from the Thirties or Forties. Cotton and wool. 28¾ x 20⅞" (73 x 53 cm.). Collection of Fifi White.

See also Wood and Osborne 1966, pls. 2-4 and O'Neale 1945, pp. 269-70.

15. Delgado 1963, p. 291, reports the use of purple, red, or black wool cords in the Fifties, which seems to be transitional from the purple of the Thirties to the black of today.
16. Described by Delgado 1963, p. 292.
17. Both uses are illustrated in Carnegie 1935, p. 158 and Marden 1947, p. 557 right.
18. Delgado 1963, p. 292.
19. An example from the early Seventies with this kind of striping, and without brocading or a randa, is in the collection of Ambassador William G. Bowdler. Another example without brocading is described by O'Neale 1945, p. 270. The Peabody Museum also has an example collected in the Thirties, with a randa and without brocading (970-24/23778).
20. Examples illustrated in use in Carnegie 1935, p. 158 and Marden 1947, pp. 551 right and 557 right.
21. Examples in the Osborne collection in the University Museum, 42-35-200 (dark blue with gauze weave), 42-35-205 (striped red, purple, and yellow).
22. See the Matilda Gray photograph published in the Handbook, vol. 6, p. 412, fig. 15.
23. Examples in the Gray collection at the Middle American Research Institute, Tulane University, G.13.3.5 and G.13.3.8.

REFERENCES

Ethnographic photographs:
Lee 1926, p. 609, women at left and right
Carnegie 1935, p. 158, women in San Pedro Sacatepéquez market (color)
Osborne 1935, p. 19, Fig. 2, woman with basket on head
Marden 1936, pl. III right, two women (color)
Muñoz and Ward 1940, p. 63, pl. 9, seated woman
Lemos 1941, p. 6 lower right, woman on the left, p. 14 top right, women
O'Neale 1945, Fig. 129a, woman with bundle on her head
Marden 1947, pp. 540, 551 (right), 557 (color)
Start 1948, pl. IIa, women in Guatemala City market (not "from Antigua")
Handbook, vol. 6 1967, p. 412, Fig. 15, cofradía altar with man and woman (Matilda Gray collection 1935)
Bunch 1977, cover illustration, seated woman in market (color)
Textiles:
Osborne 1935, pl. II no. 11, black and white belt
Lemos 1941, p. 16 top, detail of huipil
O'Neale 1945, Fig. 105 (LMO58), cofradía tzute; Fig. 122a (LMO56), woman's sash
Young 1952-3, p. 28 top, details of huipil, skirt, sash
Marks 1973, p. 8 left, huipil, with green ground
Heard Museum 1979, p. 78 (color), no. 13, woman's costume
Color renderings:
Crocker 1952, pl. 9, man and woman, plus men's cofradía
Osborne 1965, pl. 54 (1975, p. 191), man and woman
Wood and Osborne 1966, pl. 1, man; pls. 2, 3, 4, women
Petterson 1977, pp. 166-67, no. 33, woman; p. 109, no. 19, five-year-old girl
Drawings:
O'Neale 1945, Fig. 54h, man's cofradía coat; Fig. 22h, huipil stripes; Fig. 24j, huipil layout; Fig. 25a, cofradía tzute; Fig. 43c, child's huipil; Figs. 66o, 67a, 70c, k, designs
Atwater 1946, p. 34, no. 18, huipil; p. 42, no. 25, cofradía tzute
Text:
O'Neale 1945, pp. 269-70
Delgado 1963, pp. 291-93, 1957 costume
Erroneous attributions (actually San Pedro Sacatepéquez):
O'Neale 1945, Fig. 85c (Eisen's mistake)
Start 1948, pp. 28-29
Atwater 1965 ed., pl. IIIb

CHAPTER FOUR

Santiago Atitlán

Although Santiago Atitlán weaving is not as spectacular as that of other villages, the sequence of changes in the costume over the last 100 years is particularly interesting and well documented. It is the largest Indian town on the shores of Lake Atitlán with about 11,000 people in 1948. Unlike many other villages, most people live in the town. The men, in addition to farming and some fishing, make dugout canoes and rush mats, and also engage in commerce, trading highland with lowland products for the other lake villages. Many also work on the coffee plantations during the harvest months from September to December. There is a daily market, which is larger on Saturdays and Mondays. The women have their own market where they deal in local produce. Their language is Tzutujil, spoken in only a small area south of the lake.

The late 19th century costume of Santiago Atitlán is shown in Fig. 31.[1] The huipil is white with a few narrow red warp and weft stripes. It has no woven decoration but there is embroidery on the neckline, which appears to be the same as in subsequent styles. This consists of a half circle of red fabric, applied in front, with embroidery around it and embroidered points at the sides, also mainly in red. It appears to be a two-piece huipil sewn without randas, as in later examples. Also characteristic in later huipils is a hem on one end. The chief differences from later specimens are the lack of decoration apart from stripes and neck embroidery, and the use of fine red stripes instead of purple ones.

Probably around 1910-15,[2] embroidered motifs began to be added to the huipil along the shoulder line and in the front and back (see Fig. 33). These include a herringbone-like or zigzag band, and tiny geometric figures in rows. These motifs resemble those found in woven decoration in other lake villages such as Santa Catarina Palopó or San Lucas Toliman.[3] The embroidery is done in such a way that the finished effect closely resembles weaving. The yarns pass horizontally on the front of the fabric, and pass under only one warp at the edge of the design before turning back. Very little shows on the back. However, it is clear from examples in which the work slants across the wefts, and from later developments, that the decoration is definitely embroidery and not weaving. Similar embroidery is also done on men's pants in the Tzutujil village of San Pedro La Laguna.

The most conservative Santiago Atitlán huipils (those with the smallest amount of embroidery) have narrow red, purple, and orange warp stripes, spaced at 3½-4" intervals, and red weft stripes at similar or wider intervals. In the example shown, (Fig. 33), the red is 4 warps, the orange 6 warps, and the mauve 22 warps wide. Since the fabric is warp-faced, the weft stripes show much more faintly than the warp stripes. Most Santiago huipils from the Thirties have no red warp stripes, and some lack orange stripes as well. It is also characteristic of them that the half circle below the neck is made of magenta silk fabric.

Some, though not all, huipils of this period and later have some weft stripes, either in white or another color, in which a relatively heavy weft interlaces 5/1. In the example shown in Fig. 35, each stripe consists of 2 shots of 5/1 interlacing separated by one 1/1 regular weft insertion. The floats in the two heavier bands are in vertical alignment. These heavy wefts are not supplementary and there are warp floats on the back of the fabric. Such stripes are probably produced with the aid of a supplementary shed rod or heddle rod. The use of floats makes the stripe more visible on the surface than are the plain-woven red weft stripes.

Huipils of the late Forties have slightly wider warp stripes set a little closer together, and more extensive embroidery than earlier pieces.[4] Some of the embroidered motifs no longer are done with all threads parallel to the weft. Instead, small bird designs may be made with the stitches following the bird's sometimes curvilinear or diagonal outlines (see Color Plate X).

This type of huipil continued to evolve with purple warp stripes becoming still broader (and orange warp stripes eliminated) and closer together. By the mid-Sixties the purple stripes were as wide as the white ones, c. ½" (1.3 cm.).[5] The embroidery becomes still more lavish and naturalistic.[6] Something of the effect of these later pieces can be seen in Fig. 42.

At the same time, a completely different type of patterning came to be used on some huipils (Figs. 36 and 37). It developed at some time between 1950 and 1965 and involves the use of supplementary wefts. However, unlike virtually all other Guatemalan backstrap loom supplementary-weft patterning, the patterns are not picked individually by hand but are instead entirely controlled by the use of an extra shed rod and heddle rods (see Fig. 36). While up to 10 extra

No 10

Fig. 31 Santiago Atitlán men and women, late nineteenth century. Peabody Museum, Harvard University. Photograph by George Byron Gordon.

heddle rods may be used, many patterns require less. In contrast to the wide range of designs possible with hand picking, the designs possible with this type of loom control are simple, small geometric forms that repeat all across the huipil (Fig. 37). Rows of them are generally used with short plain areas between. The supplementary wefts are continuous from selvedge to selvedge. The warps to be lifted for each pattern weft are selected from those which pass over the principal shed rod and thus the patterning has the effect of being done on an open plain-weave shed and the weft, when it is not floating on the front, passes in the same shed as the ground weft and does not show on the back. Although this patterning is supplementary and thus differs fundamentally from the ribs of floats found on earlier pieces, it is possible that one evolved from the other, since the principle of loom control is similar.

The cofradía huipil is again a more conservative style (Figs. 34 and 35), normally lacking supplementary weft or embroidered patterning. Nevertheless it should be noted that in all periods some everyday huipils are also made without decoration and that the cofradía huipil is therefore not an entirely distinct type. However it is worn in the usual cofradía fashion, that is, falling loose over the skirt as seen in Fig. 34.

A number of wonderful color photographs have been published of the Santiago Atitlán women's market, showing a spectacular sea of red skirts.[7] However, these skirts only began to be worn about 1910. Previously, the Santiago Atitlán skirt was either a small blue and red checked fabric or a bold blue and white plaid such as is seen in Fig. 31.[8] The blue and white plaid fabric was woven in the Quezaltenango area on treadle looms, as is the later red fabric.[9] Both checked and plaid skirts were made of two lengths of fabric, each a complete loom width, but the red skirts are made with only a single full loom width and part of another. The ends are sewn into a tube about 10′ (3 m.) in circumference, usually by machine.[10] The red skirt has blue and white weft ikat patterning at intervals, some narrow and some broad. Some skirts also have a few narrow warp stripes.

All of the skirts are worn in the same fashion, wrapped, and with the end tucked in over the right hip. No belt is used.

The skirts of the Thirties and Forties are mostly red, but by the mid-Sixties skirts with more ikat than red were being worn.[11] By the mid-Seventies some women no longer were wearing the red skirt, but instead a skirt with polychrome weft stripes alternating with ikat stripes as in Fig. 36.[12] This type of fabric is not specific to Santiago Atitlán, as the red skirt was, but is also worn in other villages.

The Santiago Atitlán hairdress is one of the

Fig. 32 Santiago Atitlán woman, 1935. Middle American Research Institute, Tulane University, Matilda Geddings Gray Collection.

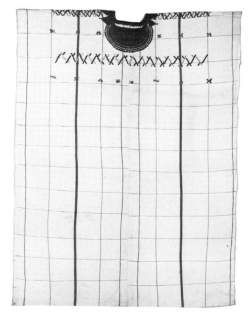

Fig. 33 Santiago Atitlán huipil, probably from the Twenties or Thirties. Cotton and silk. 45 x 33″ (1.40 x .84 m.). Textile Museum 1965.66.3.

Fig. 34 Santiago Atitlán woman in cofradía costume, 1935. Middle American Research Institute, Tulane University, Matilda Geddings Gray Collection.

Fig. 35 Santiago Atitlán cofradía huipil (detail), probably dating from the Fifties. Cotton. Collection of Fifi White.

most spectacular in Guatemala. The basic manner of doing the hair seems to have remained the same despite changes in the length and type of decoration of the ribbon. The ribbon is wrapped spirally around the length of hair which is then wrapped around the head. The remaining length of ribbon is wound around the head on top of the bound hair.[13] At the turn of the century the ribbon used was shorter and narrower than later ones, and was predominantly blue and brown in color.[14] Like later ones, however, it was woven in Totonicapán. The type with a red central section seems to have been introduced c. 1910. The central area is plain and the ends may be striped or have tapestry patterning (Fig. 38). The typical color scheme for the tapestry on older specimens such as that in Fig. 38 is orange, magenta, and green, often in a shiny rayon yarn. The length is such that when worn it stands out an inch or so from the head (Fig. 32). In the Seventies some women have been wearing ribbons that are extremely long and wrapped so that the whole arrangement slants upwards slightly.[15]

The woman's tzute has also undergone a sequence of changes. The basic form is a single loom panel of fabric with a selvedge at one end and fringe at the other end. The fringe is compactly knotted into points. Sometimes there are small tassels at the corners and center of the selvedge end. It is warp striped and only occasionally embroidered (Fig. 39). The tzute is often carried over one shoulder (Fig. 32) but may also be used as a headcloth (Fig. 31) or shawl. The oldest examples are striped mainly in natural brown cotton and dark blue, with the stripes separated by narrow white stripes. Some narrow mauve stripes may also occur. The typical tzute of the Thirties and Forties, which may also have begun to be used c. 1910, is striped in the same format, but is predominantly red and dark blue rather than brown and blue (Fig. 39). Some examples have green stripes instead of blue. By the Sixties this blue and red style was still to be seen but some women were using a tzute with ikat warps forming a bold check design,[16] and this is the style generally seen today. The ikat check design was probably borrowed from San Pedro La Laguna, as is probably the case with the men's sashes (see below).

A special tzute may be used for cofradía (Fig. 40). This tzute is usually made of two loom panels, but some examples are only one. It has a selvedge on one end and may be hemmed on the other end or have a knotted fringe. It has a different arrangement of stripes, however. It is mainly of natural brown cotton, intersected by narrow white warp stripes. Near the center are some contrasting wider warp stripes in either red or mauve.

Santiago Atitlán men's pants are made of a

Fig. 36 Santiago Atitlán woman weaving huipil fabric, mid-Seventies. She is lifting one of the supplementary heddle rods. Photograph by Marilyn Anderson.

fabric very much like the women's huipil and follow a similar stylistic development. The type of pants worn in the late 19th century may be seen in Fig. 31. They are white with narrow red stripes of warp and weft widely spaced, and without any other pattern. In length they just cover the top of the knee. They are relatively wide, and are hitched up slightly at the sides. By the Thirties (Fig. 41) they have lengthened to just cover the knee, are slightly narrower, and hang evenly. The fabric now has orange and purple warp stripes, slightly wider and more closely spaced than before. In addition, they may be embroidered in simple geometric designs similar to the women's huipil. Later examples, as shown in Color Plate X and Fig. 42, have still wider and more closely spaced purple stripes and may have more lavish embroidery including free-form birds. Many men wear striped pants without any embroidery, however. Modern pants also seem to be slightly narrower than those shown in Fig. 41 (see Fig. 43).

Although not visible in the photo in Fig. 31, the late nineteenth century man's shirt was white [17] By the Thirties, it was made of dark striped fabric, backstrap-loom woven but cut in the modern European style (see Figs. 41 and 44). The red and black striped fabric of Fig. 44 was common and was occasionally used, even fairly recently, by older men.[18] Fabric with ikat block design of the type woven in San Pedro La Laguna was also sometimes used, and such shirts have also been used by some men recently.[19] From the Forties on, however, it has been common for men to wear commercially made shirts (Fig. 43).

Early examples of men's sashes are red. They may be completely plain or have some narrow dark blue or mauve warp stripes (see Fig. 45). Some time after 1950 sashes start to have ikat stripes. The one on the left in Fig. 46 is an example of a transitional type, since the solid stripes are still red and mauve. Later sashes, such as those on the right in Fig. 46 and worn by the men in Fig. 43, have a variety of solid color stripes between the ikat ones. Again, such ikat seems to be the result of influence from San Pedro La Laguna. San Pedro weavers produced some textiles for sale to Santiago Atitlán and other places at least as early as the Thirties, so it is not surprising that such influence should occur.[20]

The older sashes have a short, closely knotted fringe on one end and newer ones have fringes on both ends. They are worn wrapped twice around the waist: wrapped front to back, crossed in back and brought to the front again where the ends are tied in a knot with a single loop.[21] The ends are allowed to hang down.

Although men have worn straw hats for some time, in the Thirties some wore a tzute, either under or

Fig. 37 Santiago Atitlán huipil, collected by Ruben Reina in 1970. Cotton. 30¾ x 26¾" (78 x 68 cm.). University Museum, University of Pennsylvania 70-13-89a.

Fig. 38 Santiago Atitlán hair ribbon, collected by Lilly de Jongh Osborne (298), probably dating from the Thirties. Cotton and rayon. 28' x 1⅛" (8.54 m. x 2.7 cm.).

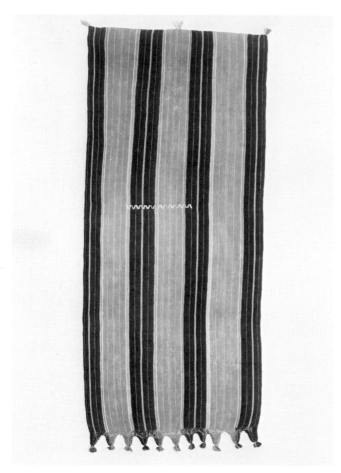

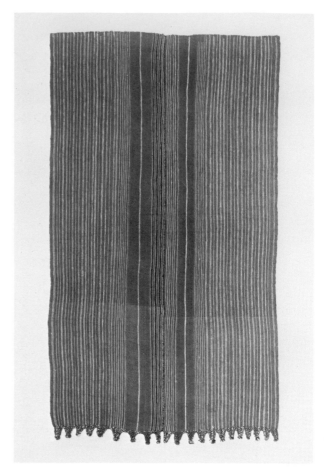

Fig. 39 Santiago Atitlán woman's tzute, collected by F.H. Lamson-Scribner in the late Thirties. Cotton and silk. 58¼ x 25⅛" (1.48 x .64 m.). Textile Museum 1964.65.42.

Fig. 40 Santiago Atitlán woman's cofradía tzute, collected by Ruth Jamison, in 1979. Cotton. 52¾ x 29" (1.34 x .74 m.).

around the hat (Figs. 41 and 47). This was a single loom panel with a selvedge on one end and a hem on the other. It was red with some brown stripes at the sides and center and with one or two mauve stripes in the center. The example shown has small magenta silk corner tassels.

The late nineteenth century style of jacket is shown in Fig. 31. This was of black and white wool with some tapestry patterning along the bottom, similar to Sololá jackets of the Thirties. This type evidently went out of use c. 1910. In the Thirties, the jacket shown in Fig. 41 was common. It was of dark blue wool, cut in the contemporary European manner. Since World War II the men have not worn jackets on a regular basis.

NOTES

1. This costume is also illustrated by the Maudslays, 1899, pp. 43, 60, plate opp. p. 62, and in Frances McBryde's watercolors, pls. 7j and k. It was still being worn by some old people in the Thirties.
2. See McBryde 1947, p. 51. Other costume innovations discussed below such as the red skirt, the long red headband, and the red and blue tzute also seem to date to this period.
3. See, for example, O'Neale, Fig. 87.
4. See Marden 1947, p. 526.
5. See Bunzl 1966, p. 90.
6. An example from c. 1970 is illustrated in the Heard catalogue, pp. 40, 74.
7. See Marden 1936, p. 44, pl. VII and the Keshishian photo on the cover of the June 1970 *Américas*.
8. The small check fabric is mentioned by O'Neale, p. 297. Both appear in Maudslay 1899, plate opp. p. 62.
9. McBryde 1947, p. 164. Some red fabric used in Santiago Atitlán was also woven in Huehuetenango. Some is now woven in Santiago Atitlán itself (see Anderson 1978, p. 158).
10. Two red skirts in the Peabody Museum, Harvard, are made in this fashion, 50-74/18256 (sewn by machine) collected in 1932 by Lothrop and 41-90/14273 (sewn by hand) collected in 1934, both of Huehuetenango fabric.
11. See for example Bunzl 1966, pp. 90, 92 and Martel c. 1975, pp. 84-85.
12. This is more clearly shown in Bunch 1977, pp. 38-39.
13. See for example Marden 1945, pp. 544-545.
14. McBryde 1947, p. 164.
15. See Bunch 1977, pp. 38-39, and Martel c. 1975, pp. 84-85.
16. See Lehmann 1961, Fig. 16; Bunzl 1966, p. 90; cover of June 1970 *Américas*; and Martel c. 1975, pp. 84-87.
17. According to McBryde 1947, p. 164; those illustrated in Maudslay 1899, pp. 45, 60, are definitely of European cut and

Fig. 41 Santiago Atitlán man, 1935. Middle American Research Institute, Tulane University, Matilda Geddings Gray Collection.

Fig. 42 Santiago Atitlán man's pants, collected by Lilly de Jongh Osborne (302), probably dating from the Sixties. 33½ x 24½" (85 x 62.5 cm.).

Fig. 43 Santiago Atitlán men, 1979. Photograph by Emily Norton; black and white from color original.

Fig. 44 Santiago Atitlán man's shirt collected by Lilly de Jongh Osborne (304). Cotton. Back: 31½ x 61″ (.80 x 1.55 m.).

Fig. 45 Santiago Atitlán man's sash collected by Mrs. Oliver Ricketson in 1932. Cotton. 60 x 8″ (52.5 x 20 cm.). Peabody Museum, Harvard University 32-37/137. Photograph by Hillel Burger.

Fig. 47 Santiago Atitlán man's tzute collected by Samuel K. Lothrop in 1932. Cotton. 26 x 22″ (66 x 56 cm.). Peabody Museum, Harvard University 50-74/18255. Photograph by Hillel Burger.

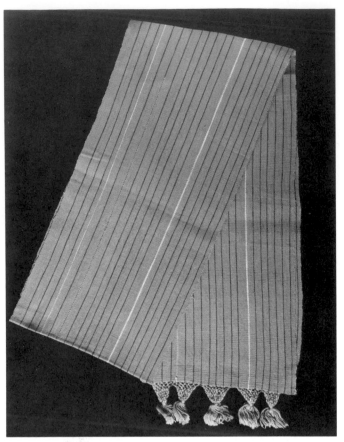

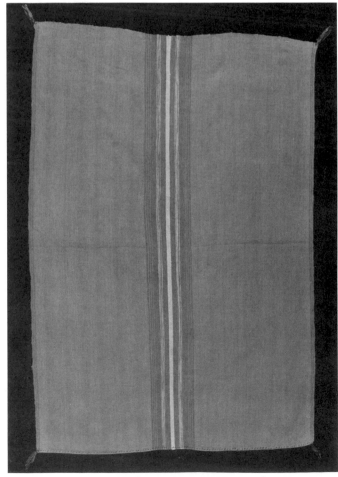

probably of commercial manufacture.

18. See Martel c. 1975, p. 88.
19. See Martel c. 1975, p. 86; Osborne 1965, pl. 23c (1975, p. 155) is an older photograph showing ikat skirts.
20. O'Neale 1945, p. 226, mentions commercial weaving of San Pedro women. Illustrations of San Pedro shawls are found in Gayer 1926, pl. IX bottom (color) and Lemos 1941, p. 5 left top.
21. The knot shows clearly in Martel c. 1975, p. 86.

REFERENCES
Ethnographic Photographs:
Maudslay 1899, pp. 45, 60 men; plate opp. p. 62 plaza
Osborne 1935, p. 27, Fig. 4, women
Marden 1936, p. 44, pl. VII market (color)
Kelsey and Osborne 1939/61, 1st, 6th, 8th plate after p. 56, 5th after p. 120
Muñoz and Ward 1940, p. 169, pl. 37; p. 176, pl. 4, woman
Lemos 1941, p. 14 top left, p. 31 top left, women
Marden 1945, pls. VI, VII, procession (color); pl. X, women carrying water (color)
O'Neale 1945, frontispiece b, woman
Marden 1947, p. 526, two standing women (color); p. 527, street scene with men and women (color); p. 542, mother and daughter, group

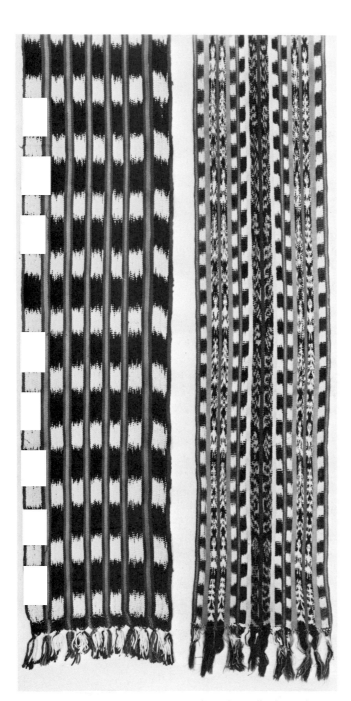

of women; p. 543, group of women (color); pp. 544-5, large group of women (color)

McBryde 1947, pl. 25f, woman carrying jar; pl. 25e, market with women spinning cotton

Lehmann 1961, Fig. 16, girl and man

Osborne 1965, pl. 2b, woman spinning cotton (1975, p. 26); pl. 4, woman weaving (1975, p. 28); pl. 7a, woman setting up the loom (1975, p. 67); pl. 15a woman (1975, p. 93); pl. 15b, group of women carrying water (1975, p. 93); pl. 23c, 2 men and woman (1975, p. 155); pl. 28b boy and girl (1975, p. 202)

Bunzl 1966, p. 90, woman; p. 92, old woman; p. 93, lower left—girl; p. 100, woman and girl washing clothes

Handbook Vol. 7, 1969, p. 38, Fig. 8 (from Osborne 1935, Fig. 4); p. 39, Fig. 9 (from McBryde 1947, pl. 25f); p. 44, Fig. 15, market scene; p. 97, Fig. 15, woman and child (Tulane)

Américas June 1970 cover—market (color)

Haba 1974, p. 665, clothesline; p. 670, women (color)

Martel c. 1975, p. 54, men; pp. 84-85, woman weaving and daughters (color) pp. 86-87, women; pp. 88-89, men

Altman 1975, Fig. 17, market (Whitman archive)

Bunch 1977, pp. 38-39, young man and woman (color)

Anderson 1978, p. 9 upper right, man; p. 31, Fig. 18, church image in ikat shawl; p. 41, Fig. 26, old woman spinning cotton

Boletin Museo Ixchel, Vol. 1, No. 8 (1979), p. 1—same as Fig. 31

Techniques:

Anderson 1978, pp. 53-56, Figs. 43-56, warping and setting up the loom; pp. 115-117, Figs, 130-134, supplementary-weft patterning; p. 158, weft ikat weaving, pp. 170-171, tapestry band weaving

Textiles:

O'Neale 1945, Fig. 107c, woman's wrap (LMO); Fig. 124b skirt fabric (LMO); Fig. 122k, man's sash (LMO)

Atwater 1965, pl. IIB skirt fabric

Tulane 1976, #24p, q, skirt and headband (color details)

Goodman 1976, pl. 14, p. 10, pants (color detail)

Anderson 1978, p. 149 lower left (color), detail of pants; p. 150 top right (color), detail of skirt fabric; p. 152 center right (color), tapestry bands; p. 181, Fig. 205, detail of pants

Heard 1979, p. 40, Fig. 8 left; p. 74 #8 and 9, man's and woman's costumes

Color Renderings:

McBryde 1947, pl. 7j, l men, 7k, m women, old and new styles (black and white), captions, p. 164

Crocker 1952, pl. 1, woman and man

Osborne 1965, pl. 61, man and woman (1975, p. 240-241), black and white

Wood and Osborne 1966, pl. 19, woman

Petterson 1977, no. 29, pl. 146

Drawings:

Maudslay 1899, p. 43, couple

O'Neale 1945, Fig. 30c, 47g, huipil; 49o, p, knotted fringes; 54i, jacket; 54m, capixay; 55t, pants; 64d jacket border; 66b4, pants design; 68b, huipil design

Text:

O'Neale 1945, pp. 296-298

Delgado 1963, p. 350, museum specimens described

Background:

Lothrop 1928a, geography and economy

McBryde 1947, historical and cultural geography

Mendelson 1958, religion and world view

Fig. 46 Santiago Atitlán sashes. Left: collected by Lilly de Jongh Osborne (303), probably dating from the Fifties or Sixties, 8'9" x 8" (2.67 x .20 m.). Right: collected by Ruth Jamison in the late Seventies, 9'8" x 7" (2.96 x .18 m.).

CHAPTER FIVE
Nahualá

Nahualá is a large Quiché-speaking town about 18¾ miles (30 km.) from Lake Atitlán. It had 21,000 inhabitants in 1948. In addition to agricultural work, the people also raise sheep and weave wool, and some also make grinding stones for sale.

The woman's huipil is large, made of two pieces of fabric, of four selvedges each (Figs. 50, 52). It has a white ground and the seams are sewn with a contrasting color of thread, now usually red (Fig. 52), though in older pieces the thread is often dark blue (Fig. 50), using small overcast stitches. The neck opening is given a T-shape, by leaving part of the center front open and by cutting a small horizontal slot at the fold. The edges of this slot are turned under and hemmed with a zigzagging stitch. To compensate for the take-up of fabric in this hem, there is a small tuck along the entire shoulder line, which is secured by a line of backstitching in the same color as the seams. The Nahualá huipil may always be recognized by this stitching even when it has no further decoration, as is not infrequently the case (see Fig. 55).

When the huipil is decorated, it is patterned with supplementary wefts on a closed plain-weave shed, so that the colored weft passes to the back of the fabric when it is not floating on the front. The work is done with the aid of a pick-up stick.[1] The designs are mostly made up of diagonal lines, so the floats are in diagonal alignment. The dominant color of the designs is usually red, though other colors may appear as accents. In many examples the weaving is extremely fine and the color effect jewel-like.

The design layout of the huipil varies slightly from one to the next but usually the decoration is concentrated toward the top. Often there is a rectangular panel across the center front and a T-shaped panel across the upper back. These features suggest that the modern Nahualá huipil is derived from a three-piece prototype, although the earliest known examples are also two-piece (see Fig. 48). These panels are usually geometrically patterned with diamond designs framed by horizontal zigzags above and below. There may also be a row of birds or animals across the top of the front or below the geometric patterning on the back. Occasionally there is a diamond-patterned band next to the arm opening. The Nahualá huipil is one of the few in Guatemala where the front and back are different (Fig. 52).

By good fortune there is a Nahualá huipil in the Eisen collection (Fig. 48). It can be seen that the design of this piece is like the later ones in all essentials, except that it is considerably simplified. The supplementary wefts are mainly red cotton, with only a little yellow added in some of the diamonds. The elaboration that is now characteristic seems to have taken place between the time the Eisen huipil was made and the Thirties (see Figs. 49-50). Also in the Thirties and later, the supplementary weft yarns were often of silk or rayon[2] although some examples do still have cotton (Fig. 50).

The deliberate use of yarns colored with a dye that will run (Fig. 52) was introduced sometime after 1940.[3] Presumably it happened unintentionally at first and some women decided they liked it. The completed huipil is now frequently soaked overnight in hot soapy water to produce the desired effect.[4]

Within the last few years, although the traditional huipil has continued to be made and worn by some, several new developments have occurred. Some huipils are made with extremely large animal or diamond patterns.[5] Other huipils are made in new color combinations, such as yellow supplementary wefts on an aqua ground. Some women have abandoned the traditional brocaded huipil entirely and wear one that is embroidered with naturalistic looking flowers.[6] The other parts of the costume have not been so much affected.

The old style of Nahualá cofradía huipil is shown in Fig. 53. Since this huipil is not mentioned in the existing literature it is not certain exactly how it should be dated. It is made of three loom panels, which seems to confirm the supposition that the everyday huipil was once of three panels also, since cofradía huipils so often are conservative in form. All the pieces have four selvedges. The seams are sewn with red thread and a round hole is cut for the neck. The ribbon binding the edge of the neck on the example in Fig. 53 is new. The ground is white and the supplementary weft patterning is done in red cotton with accents in yellow and green. A small amount of yellow and white silk is also used. The principal design is a double-headed bird very similar to the one used in Chichicastenango huipils. The horizontal zigzags below the bird and across the shoulder differ slightly from those in the everyday huipil, but the remaining motifs are similar. The bird motifs are closer in form to

Fig. 49 Nahualá woman, 1935. Middle American Research Institute, Tulane University, Matilda Geddings Gray Collection.

Fig. 48 Nahualá huipil (detail of back), collected by Gustavus Eisen, 1902. Cotton. Lowie Museum of Anthropology, University of California, Berkeley 3-38. Photograph by the author; black and white from color original.

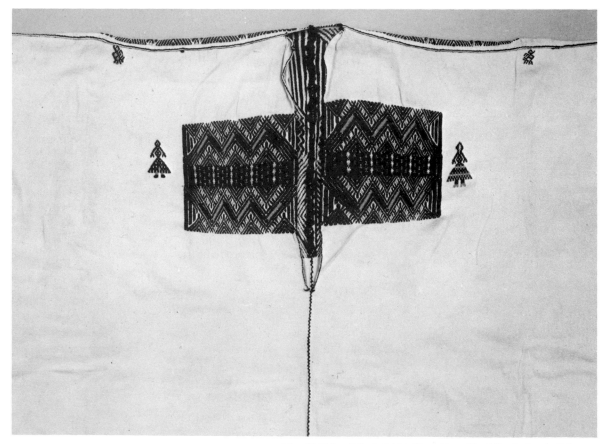

Fig. 50 Nahualá huipil (detail), collected by Lilly de Jongh Osborne before 1942. Cotton and silk. 33¼ x 40″ (84.5 x 101.5 cm.). University Museum, University of Pennsylvania 42-35-331.

Fig. 51 Nahualá family, 1980. Photograph by Susan Masuoka.

Fig. 52 Nahualá huipil: a, front; b, back; collected by Lilly de Jongh Osborne (265), probably after 1960. Cotton and silk. 34 x 44″ (86 x 102 cm.).

those on the Eisen huipil than to later huipils, an indication either of an early date for this huipil or, equally likely, conservatism in style.

The cofradía huipil is finished with lace around the neck opening and three broad pink ribbons hanging down in back, as shown in Fig. 54. This photograph also shows the modern cofradía huipil. It is still three-piece, with much deeper supplementary-weft patterning on the center than on the side panels. The side panels still have a zigzag band on the shoulder and a row of animals below. Although the central panels of the huipils in the photograph are hard to see, it is apparent that on the huipil shown fully from the back (at right) the horizontal zigzag lower border is much expanded in height and the bird almost lost in the color detailing, which has become much richer than in the earlier piece, and even more extreme than in many everyday huipils. As shown in Fig. 54, this huipil is not worn in the same way as cofradía huipils in other villages. The arms are not put through the armholes and the bottom does not hang completely free.

The skirt is made of dark blue cotton fabric woven on treadle looms in Sololá.[7] It has a pair of two-weft wide light weft stripes at 30-36" intervals. The length used is seven varas, with one vara at approximately 33".[8] The vara is an old Spanish unit of measurement, and not very precise as used in Guatemala. This length is cut in two and the two lengths are sewn together side to side and then into a tube with a narrow randa of the type in which the thread interlaces with itself between the two fabrics. The manner of putting on the skirt is shown in Fig. 55.

The woman's sash is a four-selvedge length (with the area of terminal weave in the center), dark blue with groups of narrow red warp stripes at about 1" intervals (see Fig. 56). The ends are brocaded in three or four bands of zigzag patterning similar to the huipil in magenta cotton, silk or rayon, with other colors added as accents. The sash has evidently not changed appreciably from the Thirties.[9]

Nahualá women do not make or wear a distinctive hair ribbon. Most of the time, the hair is pinned to the head without any ribbons (Fig. 51). Sometimes, for fiesta, a Totonicapán ribbon may be worn (Fig. 49).

The Nahualá woman's tzute is not highly standardized. It may be made of either one or two loom panels and is most often simply warp striped (see Fig. 57). If two-piece, the seam may be decorative. O'Neale describes the woman's tzute as blue with narrow red stripes at intervals, the typical Nahualá color pattern found also in sashes and men's tzutes.[10] However, the tzute shown in Fig. 57, which was collected in the late Thirties, has a more variegated arrangement of stripes: dark blue, yellow, natural brown, white, red, mauve, and green. Color arrangements similar to the man's tzute shown in Color Plate V are also found. The weaving is not usually as fine as on other types of textiles, even when they have brocaded patterning. Modern tzutes occur in a variety of kinds of stripings, mostly more garish than in older examples. The stripes may be wider than in the example shown.

The man's costume has changed outwardly very little in the last 100 years. There is a photograph taken by Gordon in the late 19th century which shows a group of Nahualá men wearing the black wool pullover jacket and black and white checked rodillera exactly as shown in Figs. 51 and 58. Fabrics for the jackets and rodilleras are woven locally by men on treadle looms. The manner of wearing the rodillera is shown most clearly in Fig. 58. The ends are placed in back and one or both are folded back for about a six-inch distance. It is held in place by a leather belt. The used rodillera in Fig. 59 shows where the ends have been folded back. The men wear the rodillera at all times except for cofradía as seen in Fig. 63.

Underneath, they wear a backstrap-loom woven cotton shirt and pants. The shirt is most clearly visible in the photograph of the small boy (Fig. 51) since boys do not customarily wear the wool jacket. Modern shirts are most often red with warp stripes. In the Thirties shirts were more often white (Fig. 60), though some were brown and red or blue and yellow striped.[11] The collar and the cuffs usually have supplementary-weft patterning in geometric designs similar to those of the huipil. In the modern red shirts the most usual supplementary weft color is yellow, though other colors appear as accents. In the white shirts the supplementary weft color is predominantly red, like the huipils.

The pants are most often white[12] and their construction is shown in Fig. 61. They have a cotton cord drawstring. The row of animals at the bottom is brocaded in red or purple, and in recent examples, the dye runs. The hem on the bottom of the pants is sewn with the same thread as is used for the brocading. As worn, the pants are relatively short and hitched up slightly at the sides, as can be seen in Fig. 63.

The man's sash is similar to the woman's except that the ends are decorated with a double-headed bird design framed by zigzag and diamond bands similar to the huipil (see Color Plate IV and Fig. 51). The supplementary wefts are usually either the orangy red shown in Color Plate IV, or magenta. Small boys may wear the sash outside the rodillera in place of a leather belt. Whether men wear theirs under the rodillera or only for cofradía is not clear (see Figs. 51 and 63). In any

Fig. 53 Nahualá cofradía huipil, probably dating to before 1950.
Cotton and silk. 32¼ x 35¾" (82 x 91 cm.). Collection of Fifi White.

case, it is tied in front with the ends hanging down.

The old style of the man's everyday tzute is a small squarish piece, of a single loom panel, and with corded fringes at both ends. It is either dark blue with occasional narrow red warp stripes, or a color combination such as is shown in Color Plate V. It is brocaded in silk, rayon, or cotton with small animal motifs. The brocading is usually in a variety of colors, but often magenta is dominant. The color variation seems quite arbitrary, though it is often in bands. The tzute was commonly wound around the crown of the hat (see Fig. 58) or tied around the neck. More recent examples of this same type have larger animals.

A new style of man's tzute dating at least from the mid-Sixties is shown in Fig. 62. It is longer than it is wide, and has no warp fringe. In the example shown, one end is selvedge and the other is hemmed. A fringe of contrasting color, for example yellow, may, however, be added on each end. Like the older type it has a dark blue ground fabric with narrow stripes at intervals, usually magenta. The central portion is filled with brocaded animals similar to the older type but in a variety of sizes, the larger ones quite elaborate. Unlike the older tzutes, this type also has a brocaded border all around the edge. The supplementary weft yarns used are very brightly colored cottons or

Fig. 54 Nahualá cofradía women, 1980. Photograph by Susan Masuoka; black and white from color original.

Fig. 55 Nahualá woman putting on her skirt and sash.

a The woman steps into the skirt, placing the top of the skirt above waist level. She holds the fabric out to one side, making the skirt fit tightly on the opposite hip. Still holding the fabric out with her hand, she pinches the skirt together at the hip, folding the rest of the skirt flat.

b The remaining fabric is brought around the back of the body. The far fold is held against opposite hip.

c The corner of this excess fabric is adjusted and pulled taut so that the skirt fits tightly around the waist.

d The belt is wrapped around the body once and tied in a half-hitch, with one of the belt's decorated ends close to the knot.

e The longer end of the belt is then wrapped around the waist.

f Finally, the belt's two brocaded ends are secured in a square knot. Photographs by Susan Masuoka, 1980; black and white from color originals.

acrylics, often some of each. These tzutes are used in the same manner as the older type.

For the cofradía costume (Fig. 63), a special tzute is worn (Fig. 64). It is a large white rectangle, made of two loom panels, seamed with red thread. In the center is a small rectangle of supplementary-weft patterning, mainly in red, but with some orange and yellow silk. The central design is either double-headed birds or double-headed animals (Fig. 64). The patterning is essentially analogous to the cofradía huipil. The example in the Eisen collection (1902) has two birds on each side of the seam, all surrounded by a simple border, with no further decoration.[13] Examples from the Thirties may have additional designs, consisting of little animals in the corners and around the central square.[14] Modern pieces may be very similar to these, but two of the ones in Fig. 63 have contrasting colors used as accents, creating the same jeweled effect as in recent huipils. The tzute is worn in the same way as in San Juan Sacatepéquez. It is folded in half diagonally, put over the head, and tied in back. The two white-robed men in Fig. 63 have a second tzute draped over their shoulders. The robes are European style acolyte vestments.

The shirts, pants, and sashes worn for cofradía are essentially the same as those worn daily. However, since the rodillera is not worn, the pants and sash are not hidden. Instead of the long-sleeved jacket, a short black wool capixay is worn. The sleeves of the capixay are allowed to hang free so the sleeves of the shirt are visible. Again, the use of a capixay probably represents the conservative cofradía pattern, since the jacket is more modern in form. Wide pink ribbons, like those on the women's huipils, are attached to the back.

NOTES

1. See Anderson 1978, pp. 123-125 and Sperlich 1980, pp. 99, 142-143.
2. See O'Neale 1945, p. 281.
3. It is not mentioned by O'Neale, but occurs on some men's pieces of about this date, Fig. 64.
4. Sperlich 1980, p. 142.
5. Sperlich 1980, p. 99, pl. 43.
6. This information was provided by Susan Masuoka.
7. McBryde 1947, p. 164.
8. See note 5.
9. O'Neale (1945, p. 281) does not distinguish clearly between the men's and women's sashes, although the available data suggest that the same distinction was maintained then as today.
10. O'Neale 1945, p. 281.
11. O'Neale 1945, p. 281, and McBryde 1947, p. 164.
12. Though O'Neale and McBryde, ibid., describe some pants as dark, as occurs also for shirts.
13. O'Neale 1945, Fig. 107a.
14. An example in the Textile Museum collection from the late Thirties (part of the Lamson-Scribner collection), is similar to Fig. 64 except that it has a small animal in each corner (1964.65.113).

Fig. 56 Nahualá woman's sash, collected by Leonel Beteta in the Seventies. Cotton and rayon. 7′9″ x 9⅞″ (2.38 x .25 m.).

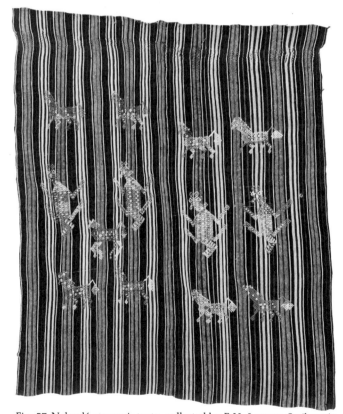

Fig. 57 Nahualá woman's tzute, collected by F.H. Lamson-Scribner in the late Thirties. Cotton and silk. 39 x 32¼″ (99 x 82 cm.). Textile Museum 1964.65.53.

Fig. 58 Nahualá men putting up a telephone pole, 1944-71. Museum of Cultural History, University of California at Los Angeles, Whitman Archive.

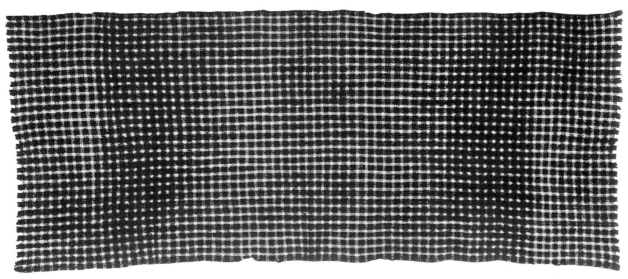

Fig. 59 Nahualá rodillera, collected by Fifi White in the late Seventies. Wool. 22 x 55¾″ (.56 x 1.415 m.).

Fig. 60 Nahualá man's shirt, collected by Matilda Geddings Gray in 1935. 41 x 26″ (1.04 x .66 m.). Middle American Research Institute, Tulane University 41-46a. Gift of Matilda Geddings Gray (Tul 40 Ma).

Fig. 61 Nahualá man's pants, collected by Lilly de Jongh Osborne (361). Cotton and rayon. 28¼ x 40¼″ (72 x 102 cm.).

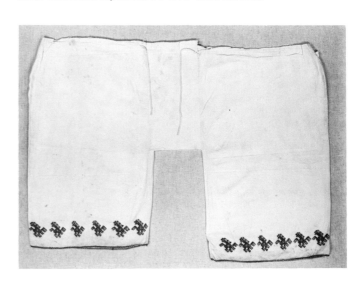

Fig. 62 Nahualá man's tzute, collected by Mrs. F.R. Fisher in 1965-66. Cotton. 33 x 19″ (83 x 48 cm.). Textile Museum 1973.11.10. Gift of Mrs. F.R. Fisher.

Fig. 63 Nahualá men in cofradía costume, Palm Sunday, 1979. Photograph by Emily Norton; black and white from color original.

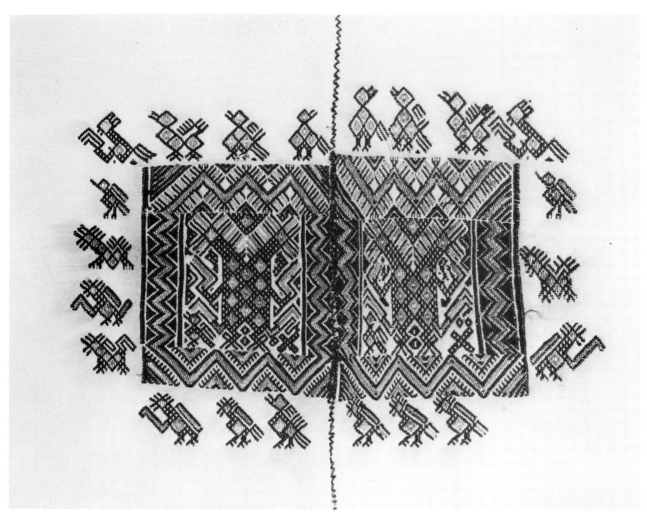

Fig. 64 Nahualá man's cofradía tzute (detail of center), collected by Matilda Geddings Gray, 1935. Cotton and rayon. Whole piece: 52½ x 49″(1.33 x 1.24 m.); central rectangle: 6 x 9½″ (15 x 24 cm.). One corner has animal. Middle American Research Institute, Tulane University 41-46d. Gift of Matilda Geddings Gray (Tul 40 Ma).

REFERENCES

Ethnographic photographs:

Osborne 1935, Fig. 1, woman shown from neck up

McBryde 1947, pl. 4d, right, men (caption for pl. 8a, p. 164)

Martel, c. 1975, pp. 72-73 (color), men

Bunch 1977, p. 58, woman praying in church (color)

Sperlich 1980, p. 72 bottom, men shearing sheep (color)

Frost 1980, p. 30 top (color), woman weaving

Techniques:

Anderson 1978, p. 124, Fig. 141, p. 125, Fig. 142, text p. 123

Sperlich 1980, pp. 43-44, pl. 20-22, setting up loom; p. 99, pl. 43, weaving; p. 142-43, pl. 68 detail, Fig. 79, weaving

Textiles:

O'Neale 1945, Fig. 107a, (Eisen), man's cofradía tzute; Fig. 107b (LMO), man's small tzute

Altman 1975, Fig. 13, tzute

Marks 1975, p. 5, left, sash

Anderson 1978, p. 118, Fig. 135, detail of front and back of huipil; p.

145, lower left (color), tzute; p. 146, bottom (color), detail of huipil

Heard Museum 1979, cover, detail of woman's sash (color); p. 36, Fig. 6 (center), detail of skirt randa; p. 57, Fig. 18, top, detail of brocaded huipil

Color Renderings:

McBryde 1947, pl. 8a, woman (caption p. 164) (black and white)

Osborne 1965, pl. 68, left, man (black and white)

Wood and Osborne 1966, pl. 24, man; pl. 25, woman

Petterson 1977, pp. 98-99, no. 17, man and woman at church; pp. 108-9, no. 19, boy and girl

Drawings:

O'Neale 1945, Fig. 55j, pants; Fig. 24e,f, huipil construction; Fig. 30d, huipil neck finish; Fig. 46d, man's tzute (LMO); Fig. 65a, 66d, 67i, motifs, tzute; Fig. 70l

Text:

O'Neale 1945, pp. 280-81

Start 1948, pp. 44-45, man's tzute

Delgado 1963, pp. 354-57, museum specimens

CHAPTER SIX
Santo Tomás Chichicastenango

The Quiché village of Chichicastenango is among the best known in all of highland Guatemala. Its market, held on Thursdays and Saturdays, attracts many vendors from distant villages, as well as tourists by the busload. The colonial church and chapel, one at each end of the market place, are also attractions. Indians burn copal incense and pray on the steps outside the church as well as inside. Near the town are stone idols which are also venerated (Fig. 80). Few of the people actually live in town; most of the municipio population of 32,500 (in 1948) come in only for markets and fiestas.

The Chichicastenango huipil is made of three loom panels, with deeper supplementary-weft patterning on the central piece than on the sides. The ground fabric is either brown or white cotton. The seaming is usually decorative, at least in part. The sides are sewn and a round hole is cut for the neck. Silk appliqué points surrounded by chain stitching frame the neckline and there are silk roundels on the shoulders and sometimes on the center front and back. Most huipils made before 1960 had a design of a double-headed bird (Fig. 66). The oldest huipils, one collected by Osborne and three collected by Eisen, show the bird more clearly than later pieces, in which the background areas are more solidly filled in.[1] Osborne's appears to be considerably older than Eisen's, since the background lacks entirely the diamond grid found in all the later pieces. Also, in all of these early huipils there is a horizontal zigzag border above the bird as well as below it, and a little blank space on the shoulder, whereas in later examples, the birds' heads are woven so close to the shoulder that they are obscured by the neck embroidery and there is no upper border. Since all three of the white-ground early huipils have blue silk appliqués, and later examples all have black appliqués, the use of blue silk seems to be another conservative feature.[2]

All of the white-ground huipils also have small animal designs in the narrow band across the shoulder on the side panels instead of the double-headed bird found (in a wider band) on later pieces. All four of these huipils have the seams sewn in a decorative zigzag stitch in blue thread. In later examples, the seams are often similar although in some examples the sections next to the central supplementary-weft-patterned area are done in a wide randa with thread

matching the brocading. All four of the early pieces have red supplementary wefts, two of silk, and two of cotton. Red cotton seems to have been the most commonly used supplementary weft yarn from 1900 to 1930 (Fig. 66), although maroon wool is also sometimes found.[3] Many of the fine Chichicastenango huipils collected in the Thirties have magenta silk supplementary wefts,[4] as does the cofradía huipil in Fig. 69. In earlier huipils, including the Eisen specimens and Fig. 66, the wings and tails of the birds are woven with vertical and horizontal bands, while in examples from the Thirties and later, zigzags are used.

In the late Forties the contrast color accents were done in stronger and more varied colors than before, emphasizing the diamond and zigzag components of the design.[5] The next step, apparently in the Fifties, was to eliminate the bird in the side panels, substituting purely geometric patterns (diamonds or zigzags).[6] Next, the geometric designs cover the central panel as well (Fig. 68).

Also in the Sixties, an entirely new type of patterning began to be used, involving a different weaving technique as well as a changed design repertory. The bird and geometric patterns had been woven with the pattern floats in diagonal alignment but the new designs are woven with the floats in vertical alignment. The reason for this change was probably to permit adapting designs from cross-stitch embroidery books, which are drawn on graph paper. The new designs are naturalistic flowers from pattern sheets of European origin (see Fig. 70 left and 80), although some geometric designs are also woven in the new technique.[7] In both cases, the supplementary weft is inserted with a closed shed, and the interlacing order is 6/2. In the older style, the warps to be lifted for each supplementary weft were selected individually with the help of a pick-up stick. In the new technique, a small extra shed rod is placed under all of the warps between the columns of design, so that all may conveniently be raised at once. The different colors for the single shed are selected with reference to the pattern. There are few rules governing colors in these huipils and even the ground fabrics may be of blue, red, green, or other hues. Acrylic yarn is often used for the supplementary wefts in both techniques. During the weaving, the floats on the front of the fabric are raised slightly by a flick of the finger, which, together with

Fig. 65 Chichicastenango woman, 1935. Middle American Research Institute, Tulane University, Matilda Geddings Gray Collection.

Fig. 66 Chichicastenango huipil, collected by Lilly de Jongh Osborne (200), probably dating from 1910-1935. Cotton and silk. 32¾ x 34½"(83 x 87.5 cm.).

Fig. 67 Chichicastenango woman, 1979. Photograph by Emily Norton; black and white from color original.

Fig. 68 Chichicastenango huipil collected in the Seventies by Leonel Beteta. Cotton and silk. 30 x 36¼"(76 x 92 cm.).

Fig. 69 Chichicastenango cofradía huipil, probably from the Thirties. Cotton and silk. 24 x 35"(61 x 89 cm.). Collection of Fifi White.

the thickness of the supplementary weft relative to the ground, creates a thick rich surface texture.

The huipil is worn with the extra fullness pulled around to the back, with the right side folded over the left. It is held in place by the belt but not tucked into the skirt (Figs. 65 and 67).[8]

The cofradía huipil (Figs. 69 and 70) is of more conservative form than the everyday one, in that the design panel is placed well below the neckline. The example in Fig. 69 is also conservative in its short design panel, with the bird not filling the loom width. It is possible that the age of this piece compares to that of men's sashes with similar design panels (see below). Examples with deeper design panels are known from the Thirties.[9] The use of the double-headed bird motif has persisted longer in cofradía huipils than in everyday huipils, but some examples now have geometric patterns, such as the zigzag in Fig. 70. As shown in this illustration, the cofradía huipil is worn loosely over the regular clothing and not tucked in. The hair style of this woman is also notable. She has red tapes wound around the tops of two locks of hair which are not braided, but hang free below. Her headcloth is not a local style but is a Quezaltenango type of shawl (compare Fig. 100).

The Chichicastenango skirt is a comparatively short one, worn about knee length. The dark blue cotton fabric is woven locally on treadle looms.[10] It is 16-18″ (41-46 cm.) wide, narrower than the 23″ typical of other areas. It has white weft stripes, four pairs of 2-weft-wide pins alternating with two groups of four closely spaced weft stripes, of which the center ones are 4 wefts wide and the rest are 2 wefts. In the example in Fig. 71 there are 10 blue wefts between groups of white ones. Some time during the Sixties ikat wefts began to be added to some skirts, in place of the wider clusters of plain white weft stripes (Fig. 72). Two 7′9″ (2.36 m.) lengths of fabric are sewn side by side and then into a tube with a broad randa. In older skirts, the sewing thread may be magenta silk; in newer ones, a brownish red (Fig. 71), with occasional bands of contrasting colors. Other colors are also used, especially in recent examples. The stitch interlaces with itself in the center between the two fabrics.[11] The skirt is wrapped smoothly around the body, the extra length passing around the back, ending on one side.

The woman's belt is of the black-and-white striped wool variety, woven by men, about 2″ (5-6 cm.) wide. It is usually embroidered for 30-35″ (76-89 cm.) on one end (see Fig. 73), again by men. Sometimes there is also about 3″ (7 cm.) of embroidery on the opposite end. The warp ends may

form a fringe, which is usually corded, or they may be finished off and more colorful yarns added as fringe (Fig. 73). Conservative belts, as on the left in Fig. 73, have only a simple pattern of five vertical columns, corresponding to the warp stripes, using dark red or magenta silk with contrasting bars of color in the central column.[12] The 5-column embroidery is actually found on all the examples shown, with the exception of the second from the left, which has an aberrant but elegant diamond design that seems to be related to vertical border patterns in woven textiles. However, in these other belts the columns are partially obscured by floral motifs. In belts from the Thirties, the flowers are relatively schematic and flat, while examples from the past decade have more naturalistic looking flowers, often in cotton rather than silk or rayon thread. The newer example illustrated had been dipped in blue dye, a common practice, although quite a lot of this coloring has now been washed out. The women wind the belts around their waists several

Fig. 70 Chichicastenango woman in cofradía costume, December 1980. Photograph by Raymond E. Senuk; black and white from color original.

times, so that the patterning shows on the outside, and the end is tucked in.

Chichicastenango women may wear their hair in a variety of ways, although usually it hangs down the back and is not pinned to the head. It may fall loose completely, or be tied together at the nape of the neck, or be braided into one or two plaits, with or without yarns or a strip of commercial fabric worked in. In the Thirties, it was common for women to bind the first 6-8" of their two braids tightly with black wool yarn.[13]

The woman's tzute, used as a headcloth, shawl, or bundle cover, is a large, approximately square piece made of two loom panels sewn together side to side with a randa and hemmed on one end. Tzutes vary in size but average about a yard (1 m.) square. They are predominantly red, but have warp

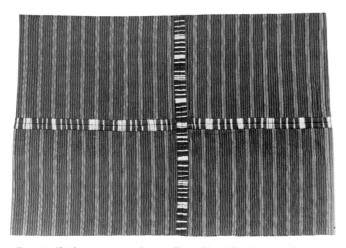

Fig. 71 Chichicastenango skirt, collected by Lilly de Jongh Osborne (201). Cotton and silk. 32½ x 46½" (.83 x 1.18 m.).

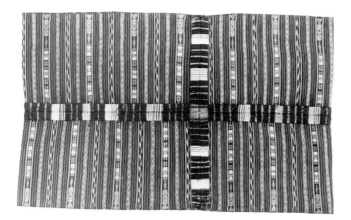

Fig. 72 Chichicastenango skirt, collected by Leonel Beteta in the Seventies. Cotton and silk. 29½ x 46¾" (.75 x 1.19 m.).

stripes in various other colors. Those from the Sixties or later may have some simple ikat stripes.[14] Most have no further decoration, but there are some elegant examples from the Thirties that have rows of brocaded animal, human, or geometric figures (Color Plate VI).

The servilleta (Fig. 74), on the other hand, seems to have been routinely brocaded. These are about half the size of the tzutes, although still made of two loom panels and hemmed on one end. Some older examples have warp stripes in white and brown. Some also have red stripes, sometimes with narrower stripes in other colors. The brocaded motifs resemble those in the tzutes and are most often done in red, though orange, yellow or pink may also be used. Although common in collections from the Thirties, they seem now to have been replaced by commercial fabrics.

The Chichicastenango man's costume was formerly worn regularly but now is worn only for cofradía. It is unusual for highland Guatemala in that it is made primarily of wool rather than cotton. The jacket and pants, of black wool, appear to be of European cut and form, but archaic—perhaps nineteenth century—in origin. The pants are knee-length and have a flap on each side (like an inside-out pocket) which has no apparent function except that it is often (though not always) embroidered with a stem with volutes around the outer edge, and with a rayed symbol in the center, in chain stitch (Fig. 76). The embroidery in the Eisen examples, especially of the rayed symbols, is simpler than in later pieces.[15] This ornamentation is often done in magenta and pink silk in older pieces, and in dark red and orange in newer ones.

The jacket occurs in two forms, one with the front cut in one piece with a centrally embroidered rayed motif, and the other with the front cut in two pieces, which are joined at the bottom, and lack the rayed motif (Fig. 75). The two-piece form is the more common one, the one-piece form being reserved for municipal officials.[16] Both Eisen jackets are of this latter type.[17] In spite of being the more prestigious form, the embroidery on these older one-piece jackets is less elaborate than on jackets of the Thirties and Forties. They lack the blue zigzags found on the cuffs, lower edge, and sometimes the shoulders of later examples. The scrolls (in red) on the sleeves and side seams are much smaller, and there is no floral or figured work. In addition, the collar bands are of blue fabric rather than of the same black wool as the rest of the jacket. A jacket collected by Lothrop in 1916-17 (Peabody Museum 17-3/C7758) is of the two-piece front type, has slightly larger scrolls than the Eisen examples, blue zigzags only on the shoulders, and no floral embroidery, so is thus transitional in style as well as date between the Eisen jackets and those from the Thirties. In jackets of the Thirties a flower on a curving stem is embroidered above the scrolls on the back, and often a small quetzal bird is embroidered on the front (Fig. 75). By the Fifties a flower might appear on the front (instead of the quetzal) as well as the back.[18] In newer examples, the flowers are usually larger and more elaborate than in older ones.

The entire construction of the jacket and pants —weaving, sewing, and embroidery—is done by men. A commercially produced European style shirt is worn under the jacket, although apparently before 1920 no shirt was worn. The outfit is completed by a sash and headcloth (tzute) woven by women in the local style on the backstrap loom.

The sash is red, and may or may not have fine dark blue warp stripes. The fringe on each end is usually corded. The one example in the Eisen collection has yellow warp stripes, and no further decoration. Though later plain ones occur, most examples in collections have some supplementary weft patterning.

In some examples, particularly earlier ones, probably before 1930, this patterning occupies a relatively narrow band at each end (Fig. 78),[19] but in most pieces from the Thirties and later, it occupies an area that is more or less square.[20] It is possible that the zigzag design on the example shown in Fig. 78 is the most conservative one for sashes,[21] although a sash collected by Lothrop as early as 1916-17 has the double-headed bird design, similar to that which appears on the cofradía huipil in Fig. 69.[22] It may be that the bird design was introduced in sashes at about this time, as it was also in the men's tzutes (see below). The zigzag design occurs again in the Fifties and later, but on a bolder scale and with polychrome wool or cotton yarns instead of dark red or purple silk.[23] By 1975, some sashes have floral designs with floats in vertical alignment similar to the newer huipils. The sash is worn twisted around the waist. It passes twice around and the ends are interlocked around each other at the front and the fringe tucked in at the sides.[24] With this arrangement, the patterned area does not show very clearly; it may be partially visible in front or slightly to the sides.

The tzute is a square formed by two rectangles sewn together with a narrow randa. Usually one end is a selvedge and the other is hemmed. A long tassel matching the supplementary wefts is attached to each corner. There are seven tzutes in the Eisen collection. Of these, five (four illustrated in O'Neale, 1945, Fig. 108) have a white ground, and two have a red ground (with narrow blue or white warp stripes). All have

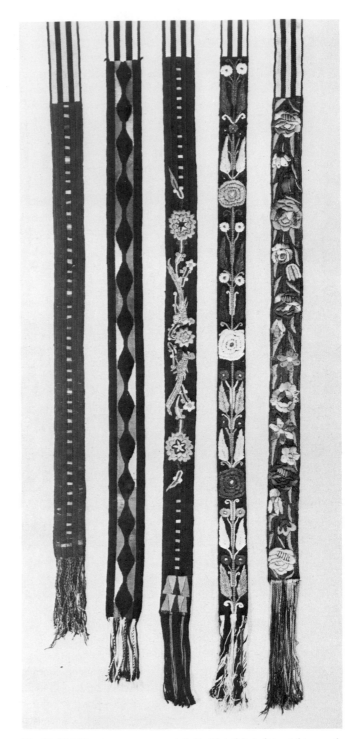

Fig. 73 Chichicastenango women's belts (details). Left to right: a, collected by Frances Toor in 1943. Wool and silk. 8′5″ x 2″ (2.57 m. x 5 cm.). American Museum of Natural History 65/4940. b, collected by Ruth Jamison in the late Seventies. Wool and silk. 8′4″ x 2¼″ (2.53 m. x 5.5 cm.). c, collected by F.H. Lamson-Scribner in the late Thirties. Wool and silk. 8′5″ x 2″(2.57 m. x 5 cm.). d, collected by Mrs. F.R. Fisher in 1965-66. Wool and silk. 8′4½″ x 1¾″ (2.55 m. x 4.5 cm.). Textile Museum 1973.11.9. Gift of Mrs. F.R. Fisher. e, collected by Ann Bowdler in 1972. Wool and cotton. 77″ x 2″ (1.96 m. x 5 cm.).

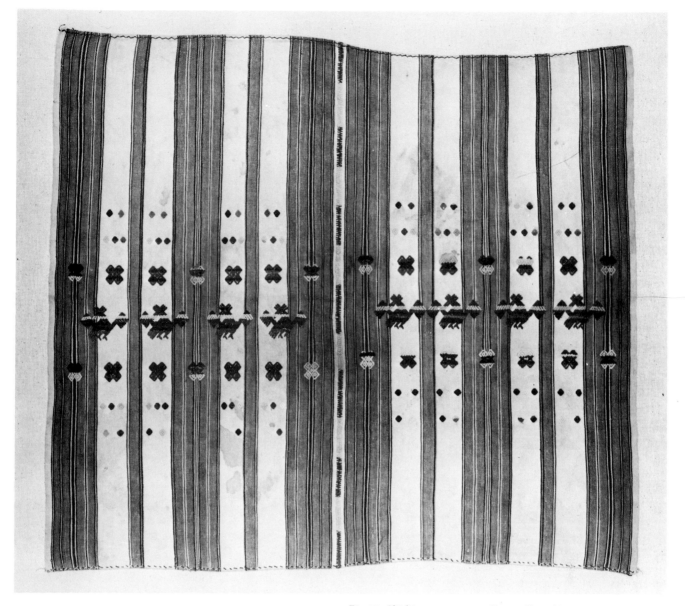

Fig. 74 Chichicastenango servilleta, collected by Lilly de Jongh Osborne (203), probably dating from before 1930. Cotton and wool. 28¼ x 32¼" (72 x 82cm.).

supplementary weft designs in a broad band across the middle, in small animal designs. The white ones have red cotton supplementary wefts and the red have yellow or yellow-orange supplementary wefts. Examples with silk supplementary wefts, usually purple (on either red or white) or yellow (on red) occur slightly later.[25] The use of the double-headed bird on tzutes, as in Color Plate XIV, also seem to have come in shortly after 1915.[26] In collections from the Thirties and Forties, red tzutes predominate, but some white ones still occur;[27] the white ones disappear entirely after 1950. From this point the stylistic changes in tzute design parallel those already described for the huipil (see Figs. 79, 80).

To wear the tzute, it is folded in half diagonally, with the fold low over the forehead. The two ends at the extremities of the fold are tied over the ends that hang down in back. The tassels often hang down in back; sometimes those from the tied corners hang down in front. Often the tzute is worn with the wrong side of the weaving facing out, presumably to protect the right side. For certain religious functions, the tzute is removed from the head and draped over the shoulders.[28]

For carrying small items, the man uses a bag (Fig. 81) with a shoulder strap which is made with plain white cotton string in warp-faced plain weave. It has not changed appreciably over the years and is generally carried over one shoulder, as shown in Fig. 75. The length of the shoulder strap can be adjusted by means of a loop at one side, to which the strap is tied. This bag is still in common use.

The man in Fig. 75 has his blanket draped over the bag, a common method for carrying it. The blanket (see Fig. 82) measures about 1 x 2 yards, and has fringed ends. It is woven of wool on treadle looms. The weave of the central black area is 2/2 twill. The design on the ends is woven in dovetailed tapestry technique, in which colored wefts, interlacing 2/2 plain weave in this case, pass back and forth within each design area. The wefts are closely enough spaced in this section to hide the warps. The blanket is used to pad the back for carrying loads, for warmth, and for decoration. It is now seen less frequently than in the past. Early examples, such as those in the Eisen collection, had some white wefts in the central section for a checked effect,[29] but later ones are solid black in the center.

NOTES

1. Osborne's huipil, University Museum 42-35-21, is illustrated by Goodman 1976, p. 16, pl. 26 in color. Two of Eisen's huipils are illustrated by O'Neale 1945, pl. 90a, b. (The third is in the American Museum of Natural History 65/3274).
2. O'Neale states in her caption that the silk appliqués in p. 90a are black. They appear to me (on actual examination of the piece) to be dark blue. Those in pl. 90b are black.
3. See Osborne 1935, pl. II, no. 2 for a color illustration. Huipils with maroon wool supplementary wefts collected in the early Thirties are in the Peabody Museum, Harvard 32-37/161, 41-90/14290.
4. For a color illustration, see Goodman 1976, pl. 30, a piece in the University Museum collected by Osborne, or Tulane 1976, no. 7h, Gray collection.
5. See Marden 1947, p. 555; Goodman 1976, pls. 1 and 2.
6. See Scofield 1960, p. 412.
7. This change has been extensively reported in the existing literature. See especially Bjerregaard 1977, pp. 55-58; Anderson 1978, pp. 135-37; and Sperlich 1980, pp. 104-06.
8. See also Goodman 1976, p. 5, pl. 2.
9. See Rodas and Hawkins 1940, Fig. 32, 33 (in Rodas 1938, p. 84, Fig. 27, p. 86, Fig. 28, p. 87, Fig. 29); Muñoz and Ward 1940, p. 162, pl. 33.
10. O'Neale (1945, pp. 53-54, 55) describes such a shop.
11. O'Neale 1945, Fig. 81 l, m, and Goodman 1976, p. 66, randa A, B.
12. cf. O'Neale 1945, pl. 122 d, e.
13. See Carnegie 1935, p. 161 for photograph; O'Neale (1945, p. 257) describes this style as then current.
14. See, e.g., Heard 1979, pp. 4-5.
15. See O'Neale 1945, Fig. 57a, d. She also points out that the Eisen specimens do not conform to the conventions described by Rodas, in which the design used supposedly reflects the age of the wearer. Indeed, the jackets that go with the Eisen pants are the type worn by municipal officials (see below) and the pants should reflect comparable status. Rodas notes that at the time of writing, the conventions for pants embroidery he describes were not followed.
16. This fact is mentioned not only by Rodas, but also by O'Neale's informant (1945, p. 213). It is confirmed by Marden's photograph (1947, p. 554) in which the leading cofrade has this type of jacket.
17. See O'Neale 1945, pp. 212-13, Fig. 57b, c.
18. Young 1953, p. 26 top.

19. Besides the one shown in Fig. 78, early sashes with narrow bands of supplementary-weft patterning include Peabody Museum 17-3/C7757 (collected by Lothrop 1916-17) and Textile Museum 1964.65.80 and 1964.65.87 (collected in the late Thirties). All three have the double-headed bird design.
20. Tulane 1976 no. 7b is an example from the Thirties, though the illustration shows only the lower part of the design and the fringe is unfinished. A later piece with a different design is in Heard 1979, p. 72 bottom (the model in this photograph does not wear the sash correctly).
21. See Rodas and Hawkins 1940, p. 113.
22. See note 19.
23. See Young 1953, p. 26 top left; Heard 1979, p. 72 bottom: a 1970 sash with zigzag of larger size and differing in other details from the 1953 example.
24. Shows clearly in Osborne 1965, pl. 26b (Osborne 1975, p. 158).
25. Lothrop collected several in 1916-17: Peabody Museum 17-3/C7760; 17-3/C7766, a group of four tzutes. Of the five, one is white and four are red. The white one has red cotton supplementary wefts, and one of the red ones is also brocaded in cotton. The rest are brocaded in yellow and purple silk. All have small animal designs.
26. This date is suggested in a note by Lothrop to accompany a tzute collected by him for the Peabody Museum (33-41/338) and is confirmed by their absence in the Eisen collection and in

Fig. 75 Chichicastenango man, 1935. Middle American Research Institute, Tulane University, Matilda Geddings Gray Collection.

Fig. 76 Chichicastenango man's pants, collected by Lilly de Jongh Osborne (209). Wool and silk. 23¼ x 35″ (59 x 89 cm.).

Fig. 78 Chichicastenango man's sash (detail), collected by F.H. Lamson-Scribner in the late Thirties. Cotton and silk. 9′2″ x 14½″ (2.80 x .37 m.). Textile Museum 1964.65.62.

Fig. 77 Chichicastenango man's jacket, collected by Lilly de Jongh Osborne (209). Wool, cotton, and silk. 22½ (center back) x 57½″(sleeve end to sleeve end) (57 x 146 cm.).

Fig. 79 Chichicastenango man's tzute, collected by Leonel Beteta in the Seventies. Cotton and silk. 33 x 35½″ (84 x 90 cm. excluding tassels).

Fig. 80 Chichicastenango man, 1970s. Photograph by Rodolfo Reyes Juarez.

Fig. 81 Chichicastenango man's bag, collected by F.H. Lamson-Scribner in the late Thirties. Cotton and wool (tassels). 16⅜ x 16⅛″ (41.5 x 41 cm.) (excluding strap). Textile Museum 1964.65.136.

Fig. 82 Chichicastenango man's blanket (detail), probably dating from the Fifties. Wool. 8′ x 26¾″ (2.385 x .68 m.). Textile Museum 1963.10.6.

Lothrop's own collection from 1916-17 (see note 25) and presence in later collections. In the Lowie Museum are two tzutes collected in 1923-25 which have the double-headed bird design, one in purple silk (3-23459) and one in black cotton (3-23460), both on red grounds.

27. In Marden's 1947 photograph (p. 554), only two of the eighteen men have white tzutes, and all have the double-headed bird design except one of the white ones, which has small animals.
28. See, e.g., Heard 1979, p. 19 top.
29. O'Neale 1945, Fig. 127. Two blankets collected by Lothrop in 1916-17 also have white weft stripes (Peabody Museum 17-3 / C7772 and C7774).

REFERENCES

Note: the photographs in Rodas (1938) and Rodas and Hawkins (1940) are not listed individually here since all illustrate Chichicastenango.

Ethnographic photographs:
Gayer 1926, pl. II men; pl. III right, men; pl. IX top, men; pl. X, market; pl. XVI, woman (color)
Lee 1926, p. 644, funeral
Osborne 1935, p. 31 (right), Fig. 5, standing woman
Carnegie 1935, p. 161, woman weaving servilleta, back view; p. 162, man
Long 1936, p. 430, man carrying pottery; p. 434 bottom, woman feeding pig; p. 453 bottom, mask maker
Marden 1936, pl. V color, top, men on church steps, bottom, three men and woman praying
Kelsey and Osborne 1939 / 1961, 2nd plate after p. 56, 1st, 2nd, 8th plate after p. 120, men
Muñoz and Ward 1940, p. 135, pl. 25, male officials; p. 137, pl. 26, women in market, p. 145, pl. 27, man and girl at mountain shrine; p. 152, pl. 29, men on church steps; p. 155, pl. 30, inside church; p. 160, pl. 31, men; p. 161, pl. 32, male cofrade; p. 162, pl. 33, men and women cofrades; p. 197, pl. 48, woman spinning; p. 232, pl. 57, man and woman
Lemos 1941, p. 5 lower left, woman; p. 7, second from bottom, church steps; p. 13, woman weaving; p. 14, bottom, man; p. 18, center and bottom right, woman weaving; p. 33, top center and center left and right, musicians
Marden 1945, pl. I color, church with many in costume; pl. III color, church steps, burning incense
O'Neale 1945, Fig. 130e, family; 130f, man in profile
Marden 1947, p. 553 (color), church steps; p. 554 (color), male cofrades; p. 555 (color), woman weaving; p. 556 (color), road to market
McBryde 1947, pl. 17e, man and three small girls; pl. 28, market from above; pl. 29a, market, 29b, male cofrade and woman
Scofield 1960, p. 412 (color), woman grinding corn; p. 413 (color), mask maker; p. 414 (color), church and market; p. 415 (color), inside church
Lehmann 1961, Fig. 14, women; Fig. 17, men
Osborne 1965, pl. 17c (1975, p. 127), woman, photograph by McBryde; pl. 26b (1975, p. 158), men; pl. 27a (1975, p. 201), family; pl. 28a (1975, p. 202), mother and daughter; pl. 34a (1975, p. 276), men on church steps
Bunzl 1966, p. 2 top (color), woman weaving; p. 42, woman; pp. 36-37, women on church steps; p. 99, woman
Handbook 1967, vol. 6, p. 307, Fig. 4, man and woman, Tulane photograph; 1969, vol. 7, p. 92, Fig. 14, man praying, 1948 photograph by Rodas; p. 41, Figs. 11, 12, women at market
Marks 1976, Fig. 1, man
Fay 1975, p. 754 (color), woman burning incense
Martel, c. 1975, p. 70, woman; p. 93, men; p. 97, market (see also pp. 95, 104-105); p. 99, church steps, and carrying image (color)
Altman 1975, Fig. 12, market (Whitman archive)
Goodman 1976, pl. 1 (color), woman weaving; pl. 2 (color), standing woman (back view); pl. 3 (color), men (cofrades); pl. 4 (color), woman sewing a randa (pls. 1, 2, 4 probably older)
Bjerregaard 1977, p. 55 old woman; p.56 men; pl. 16 (color) women
Bunch 1977, p. 63 (color) man and woman
Petterson 1977, p. 84, Fig. 7 (color) church steps; p. 116, Fig. 8 (color) procession
Anderson 1978, p. 178, Fig. 199 woman making skirt randa
Reina and Hill 1978, opp. p. 207, pl. VIII (color) women in market
Heard 1979, pp. 4-5 (color) women in market; p. 19 top (color), cofrades

Techniques:
O'Neale 1945, pp. 59, 61, brocading; p. 73, technique for weft loop pile; pp. 81-82, embroidery; pp. 209-10, blanket weaving
Bjerregaard 1977, pp. 55-58, old and new brocading
Anderson 1978, pp. 135-37, Figs. 152-56, brocading
Sperlich 1980, pp. 104-06, Figs. 44-46, pl. 46 (Chiché)

Textiles:
Osborne 1935, pl. I color (center right), servilleta; pl. II color, no. 2, top of huipil (red on white)
Lemos 1941, p. 22 upper left and lower right, men's tzutes; p. 25 no. 7, huipil, and no. 4, woman's tzute (color); p. 35 center, servilleta
Breuer 1942, no. 28, man's tzute (1937)
O'Neale 1945, Fig. 108a-d, white ground men's tzutes (Eisen); Fig. 90a, b, huipils (Eisen); Fig. 110a, b, servilletas (LMO and Eisen); Figs. 115a, 117a, items with weft loop pile (LMO); Fig. 118i, headband (Eisen); Fig. 121f, man's sash (Eisen); Fig. 122d, e, women's belts (LMO, Eisen); Fig. 126, man's jacket (LMO); Fig. 127, man's blanket (Eisen)
Young 1953, p. 29 top, jacket, sash; p. 27 top, man's tzute; p. 28 below, huipil, belt, skirt
Sowards 1974, p. 1, huipil (TM, acquired 1945)
Goodman 1976, p. 16, pl. 26 (color), old huipil (University Museum); pl. 30 (color), huipil (University Museum); pl. 18 (color), servilleta (University Museum, same as Osborne 1935); pl. 20 (color), two men's tzutes (Met); pl. 32 (color), man's pants (Met); p. 73, detail of man's jacket (Met)
Tulane 1976, no. 7b, f-h, j, l (color), huipil, skirt, belt, man's pants, jacket, sash
Bjerregaard 1977, no. 13 (color), new huipil
Siskin 1977, Fig. 1, new huipil
Anderson 1978, p. 136, Fig. 154, huipil; p. 183, Fig. 208, men's pants; p. 149, lower right (color), market stall
Heard 1979, p. 43, Fig. 10 top (color), huipil; p. 69, Fig. 25 (color) detail, men's costume; p. 72 bottom, man's and woman's costumes on models

Color Renderings:
McBryde 1947, pl. 8b, man, 8c, woman (black and white), caption pp. 164-65
Crocker 1952, pl. 12, man and woman
Osborne 1965, pl. 58, man and woman
Wood and Osborne 1966, pl. 32, man; pl. 33, woman
Petterson 1977, pp. 86-76, no. 15, woman; pp. 88-89, no. 16, market (before 1960)

Drawings:
Maudslay 1899, color plate no. 2, left—servilleta, right—man's tzute
O'Neale 1945, Fig. 24 l, o, huipil; Fig. 43a, d, h, children's huipils; Fig. 52w; skirt, Fig. 54d, jacket (Eisen); Fig. 55b, pants; Fig. 57a-d, jacket and pants (Eisen); Fig. 57e, belt; Fig. 58d, f, bag (LMO); Figs. 71e, 72d, designs; Fig. 84e, man's tzute; Fig. 63b, blanket
Atwater 1946, p. 40, no. 23, woman's tzute (note: p. 42, no. 25 is San Juan Sacatepéquez)
Start 1948, pp. 46-47, Fig. 18, woman's tzute

Text:
Maudslay 1899, pp. 72-74
Rodas 1938, pp. 31-118, symbolism on textiles
Rodas and Hawkins 1940, pp. 103-46, symbolism on textiles
Muñoz and Ward 1940, pp. 190-96, costumes
O'Neale 1945, pp. 256-58, costume, plus many other brief references including pp. 191-92, pants; pp. 212-13, jackets; pp. 206-07, men's tzutes
Start 1948, pp. 25-26, huipil; pp. 44-46, man's tzute
Delgado 1957, p. 333, museum specimens described

Background:
Rodas 1938, pp. 5-28, 123-46
Ricketson 1939, municipal organization
Rodas and Hawkins 1940, pp. 3-100
Bunzel 1952, ceremonial customs

CHAPTER SEVEN

San Miguel Totonicapán

Totonicapán, the capital of the Department of Totonicapán, is a large town with a substantial Ladino as well as Quiché population totaling 33,000 in 1948. Various kinds of craftwork are produced commercially and sold there, including glazed pottery made with traditional Spanish techniques, and pine furniture, as well as various kinds of textiles. Woolen goods, skirt fabrics, hair ribbons, and huipil fabrics are all made on treadle looms, and women's belts on the backstrap loom. All of these kinds of textiles are marketed widely throughout Guatemala. It is not the purpose of this chapter to describe this production in detail, however, but rather to present some information about the costumes actually worn in Totonicapán.[1]

Totonicapán men have not worn a handwoven costume for many years, but at the turn of the century they still wore a special costume for cofradía that has some links with traditional dress (see Figs. 83-84 and Color Plate IX).[2] The basic elements of this outfit, a white shirt and pants with wool jacket and overpants split to the thigh, were characteristic men's cofradía costumes in numerous other villages at that time, although the overpants of Totonicapán are especially lavishly decorated.

For comparison with the examples at hand, there are three pairs of overpants and a jacket in the Eisen collection at the Lowie Museum of Anthropology.[3] Two of the Eisen overpants have a black wool ground, and the third is green cotton-backed velvet. The Osborne example (Color Plate IX), which she labeled as used by the Cofradía de la Santisima Trinidad, is made of a heavy black satin fabric. All are lavishly embroidered in silk with floral patterns, although the workmanship of the Osborne pants shows more finesse than the Eisen examples. The zigzag of black fabric with pink underlining and the row of silver balls on the opening edges of the pants are found in all examples.

The same balls and silver plaques are found on the jacket. The front of the jacket in Fig. 84 is identical to those in Fig. 83. It is of navy blue wool and basically European in cut though, like many Guatemalan jackets of that period, it is a pullover, rather than being open in front. The sleeves have been turned in the illustration to show the attachment of the balls on the front. The jacket in the Eisen collection is similar, although it is made of black rather than blue wool.

Also illustrated here is one of the sarapes that Eisen bought in Totonicapán from the same man who sold him the jacket and overpants, whom he names as "Martoom." This is simply a title for an official in the cofradía. The sarape is one of a number of items in the Eisen collection which was exchanged with the American Museum of Natural History in New York in 1907, and therefore was not studied or mentioned by O'Neale.[4] These sarapes are curious since they so closely resemble Mexican ones in design and execution. They are woven in slit tapestry weave on treadle looms. However, Eisen states definitely that they were made in Totonicapán, some 20 years before, though by only a single family. The resemblance to Mexican examples is more striking in a black and white illustration than it is when actually looking at the examples. The Totonicapán sarapes are much thicker and less flexible than most of their Mexican cousins of the same date. A variety of very gaudy aniline colors was used. It is possible that a Mexican piece had found its way to Guatemala and was there copied and used for inspiration by Guatemalan weavers. Although Eisen says that the sarapes were used by the cofradías, it is not clear what their exact function was.

The photograph in Fig. 86 may well illustrate the late nineteenth century woman's costume from Totonicapán. The huipils do not show clearly enough to permit certain identification, although there are a number of Totonicapán huipils in the Eisen collection which can be used for comparison.[5] They are at any rate made of two loom panels and decorated with crossbands of different sizes, some plain and some patterned, as in the later example shown in Fig. 87.[6] They are woven locally on treadle looms. The plain stripes in Fig. 87 are red, green, and yellow, and are woven in a weft-faced 3 / 1 broken twill with the weft-float face on the front,[7] a device also found on some of the Eisen huipils.[8] The brocading is done on a plain weave ground. The supplementary wefts interlace 3 / 1, with the floats in either vertical or alternating alignment.

Since two of Eisen's Totonicapán huipils are backstrap-loom woven and their designs resemble some of the treadle-loom woven ones, O'Neale suggests that a transition from backstrap to treadle loom weaving was taking place at or before the time of Eisen's visit in 1902.[9] However, a different interpretation of the data is even more plausible. Since the

Fig. 83 Totonicapán men in cofradía costume, c. 1900. From an old postcard.

backstrap-loom woven huipils are virtually identical to huipils that Eisen collected from San Martín Jilotepeque,[10] it is likely that these Totonicapán huipils were woven there. Many huipils from San Martín occur in turn-of-the-century collections and it appears that many were made for sale. The ones Eisen collected in Totonicapán have been altered to conform more closely to the local treadle loom style. They have an extra length of commercial white fabric sewn to the bottom and have neckline finishes similar to the treadle-loom woven examples. The design similarities can still be explained as the treadle loom weavers' imitations of San Martín Jilotepeque style, since the San Martín huipils were clearly a marketable commodity. The designs of other treadle-loom woven huipils differ from the imitation San Martín ones. The designs of the huipils in Fig. 86 resemble this latter kind rather than the San Martín Jilotepeque examples. Totonicapán huipils were made for sale as well as for local use, and Osborne's tag indicates that the huipil in Fig. 87 was actually used in Mixco, a town where no weaving was done by the Thirties, although the cofradías dressed in huipils of handwoven fabrics bought from such places as San Martín Jilotepeque, San Pedro Sacatepéquez and Quezaltenango, besides Totonicapán.[11]

The modern Totonicapán huipil is shown in Fig. 88. It is made of a single width of fabric, with a square hole cut in the center for the head. A separately made embroidered neckband is applied. The fabric is so wide that vertical tucks are taken over the shoulders. The character of the patterning has also changed. Some examples have bands of small geometric designs separated not by twill stripes but by supplementary-weft bands, with the floats vertically aligned.[12] Other examples, such as the one in Fig. 88, have no separating bands and have animal designs which resemble Quezaltenango weaving. These huipils are woven on the draw loom, an elaborate type of treadle loom, with which complicated designs can be controlled by the loom apparatus.[13]

The skirts worn by the women in Fig. 86 have weft ikat patterning. Ikat skirt fabrics are now very widely used but in the late nineteenth century they were not nearly as common. However, since ikat skirt fabric is made in Totonicapán as well as in several nearby areas, it is logical that it would be worn there even at such an early date. In the Thirties both weft ikats and double ikats were worn.[14] The same seems to be true today.[15] The skirt fabric shown in Fig. 89 is the type of double ikat made in Salcajá (on the road between Totonicapán and Quezaltenango), which is the most ubiquitous type of ikat skirt fabric. The skirt

worn by the woman in Fig. 88 is this type of fabric. Part of it is just visible next to her right forearm, and the rest is covered by her apron, which is also of ikat material. The skirt is worn wrapped, with the end coming toward the front from the back, as shown in Fig. 86. The second fold in front (on the right in Fig. 86) is a smaller pleat of fabric.[16]

The belt used (Fig. 90) is the type locally woven on backstrap looms, which is also widely exported. This type of belt seems definitely to be the one used in Fig. 86. It is woven with black and white warps alternating. While one color of warps interlaces 1/1, the other interlaces 3/1 in alternating alignment. Since the belt is warp-faced, the three-span warp floats form the design areas, some of which are accentuated with supplementary wefts of contrasting color under the floats. The loom is set up so that three-span floats of either color in either of the two alternating positions can be formed, but the individual designs are made by selecting from the yarns of one or two of these four sheds with a pick-up stick. The white warps are con-

Fig. 84 Totonicapán cofradía jacket, collected by Lilly de Jongh Osborne (44d), probably dating from c. 1900. Wool. 24¾ x 18½" (62.5 x 47 cm.).

trolled by two heddle rods, each of which controls alternate white warps. The black warps are controlled by the shed rod, and the alternate warps by a second shed rod and another heddle rod.[17] The belt is worn in the same way as in other towns, wrapped several times around the waist with the ends tucked in.

Totonicapán women have not and still do not generally wear the tapestry-woven ribbon that is made in the town for export. From the Thirties on at least, the most common hair style has been simply to wear two braids down the back, as seen in Fig. 88. The style shown in Fig. 86 is therefore all the more fascinating. A ribbon is braided into the hair and the ends tied above the forehead. The ribbon appears to be completely plain.

No single type of shawl is characteristic of Totonicapán. The shawl shown in Fig. 86 has fine warp ikat patterning and a loosely knotted fringe. The type of shawl associated with Totonicapán in the Thirties is of a markedly different type (Fig. 91). It is made of two widths of treadle-loom woven fabric, hemmed at both ends. The weaving is weft-faced, and there are weft stripes in red, yellow, green, natural-brown cotton, and indigo ikat. In some examples the color palette is more restricted than in others, and the width of the stripes and the complexity of the ikat varies also. There are few photographs showing this type of shawl being worn. It was apparently worn both as a headcloth and a carrying cloth, as well as a shawl.[18]

Today, a warp ikat shawl of the same type used in Quezaltenango (compare Figs. 88 and 100) is most commonly seen. These shawls are of a single loom width and have the fringed ends knotted.[19]

NOTES
1. See the list of references under "Techniques" for further information about production weaving in Totonicapán.
2. The photograph in Fig. 83 is also reproduced in Osborne 1965, pl. 30a (1975, p. 214).
3. Described by O'Neale 1945, pp. 192-93, 216, though her text does not make clear that these overpants are from Totonicapán. They were in fact acquired in Totonicapán by Eisen and exactly match the Osborne examples in style.
4. She discusses the other four sarapes on pp. 215-16.
5. O'Neale 1945, Figs. 95a-c, 96b, c, 97a.
6. Closely resembles the example from the Thirties in O'Neale 1945, Fig. 96a.
7. See Emery 1966, p. 103.
8. O'Neale 1945, p. 73, Fig. 96c.
9. O'Neale 1945, p. 67; one of the backstrap loom huipils is illustrated in Fig. 95c.
10. Some are illustrated in O'Neale 1945, Fig. 86. Both the Totonicapán ones have a dark green ground, and so does one from San Martín Jilotepeque collected by Eisen now in the American Museum of Natural History (65/3280).
11. The huipil with Gray's Mixco costume was woven in Quezaltenango (Tulane 41-68a). See Handbook vol. 7, p. 76, Fig. 5.

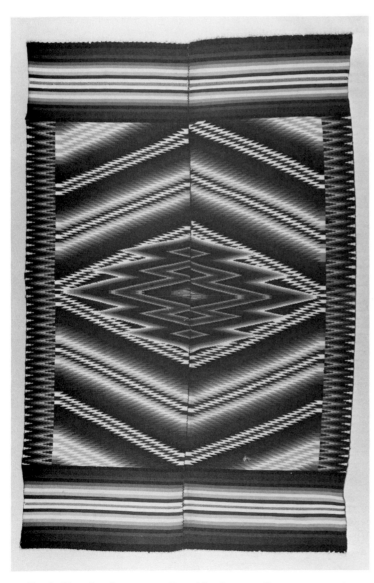

Fig. 85 Totonicapán sarape, collected by Gustavus Eisen, 1902. Wool and cotton. 81 x 52" (2.06 x 1.32 m.). American Museum of Natural History 65/3258.

Fig. 86 Men and women, probably from Totonicapán, late nineteenth century. Peabody Museum, Harvard University. Photograph by George Byron Gordon.

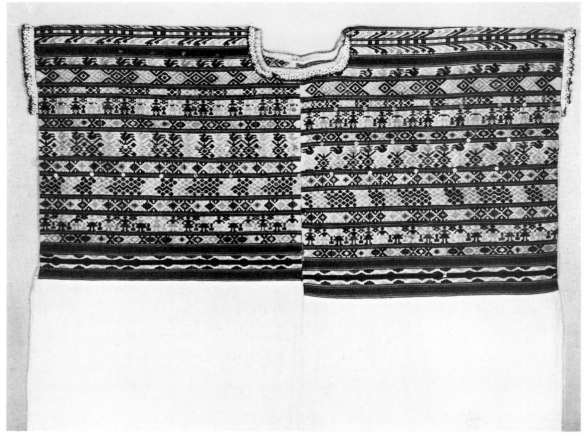

Fig. 87 Totonicapán huipil, collected by Lilly de Jongh Osborne (40), probably dating from the Thirties. Said to have been used in Mixco. Cotton, silk, and sequins. 33½ x 40½ " (85 x 103 cm.).

Fig. 88 Totonicapán woman, mid-Seventies. Photograph by Marilyn Anderson.

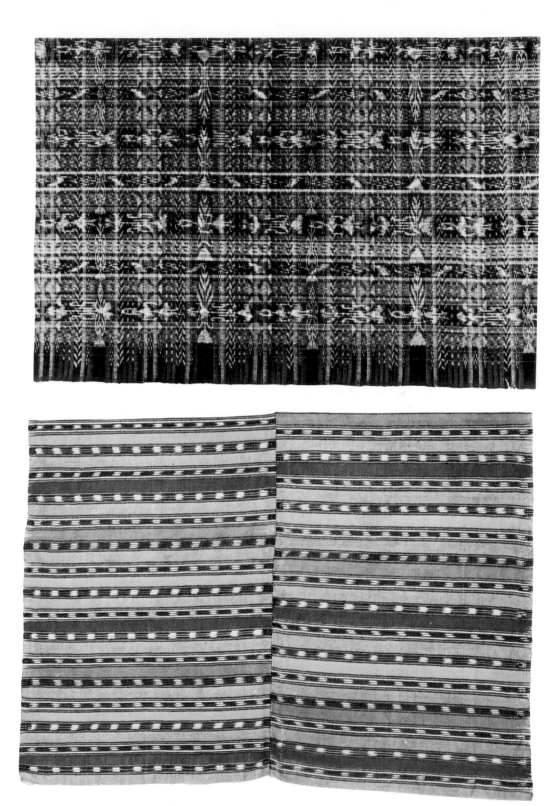

Fig. 89 Skirt fabric (detail) made in Salcajá, but used in Totonicapán and elsewhere. Collected by Lilly de Jongh Osborne (29). Cotton. Loom width: 37¾″ (96 cm.) (side selvedge at bottom).

Fig. 91 Totonicapán woman's shawl (detail), probably dating from before 1940. Cotton. 76¾ x 41″ (1.95 x 1.04 m.) (overall). Collection of Ruth Jamison.

12. See Anderson 1978, p. 152 center left, p. 164, Fig. 183, for examples.

13. See Anderson 1978, pp. 163-67.

14. A weft ikat skirt is shown in Wood and Osborne 1966, pl. 50. Double ikats in Start 1948, pl. IA, VIB; O'Neale 1945, Fig. 129c.

15. Anderson 1978, p. 8 lower right, shows a woman in a weft ikat skirt, fabric of the type woven in San Cristóbal Totonicapán (p. 59, Fig. 176).

16. See also Wood and Osborne 1966, pl. 50; Anderson 1978, p. 8 lower right.

17. See Anderson 1978, pp. 142-44. This set-up is the same as that in Osborne's drawing (1965, Fig. 10d, 1975, p. 66).

18. See Long 1936, p. 431—her headcloth lacks ikat patterning but is clearly of the general type described. Her huipil is of the same type as Fig. 87 here. The woman in Start 1948, pl. IA is carrying her baby in a shawl that has a predominance of ikat patterning.

19. The end of the shawl in Fig. 88 may be seen in Anderson 1978, p. 9 top center.

REFERENCES

Ethnographic photographs:

Long 1936, p. 431, woman

Muñoz and Ward 1940, p. 223, pl. 54, woman

O'Neale 1945, Fig. 129c, women

Start 1948, pl. IA, woman

Osborne 1965, pl. 30a (1975, p. 214), men, cofradía

Anderson 1978, p. 8, lower right, man and woman; p. 9 top center, woman

Techniques:

O'Neale 1945, pp. 37, 53, 151-55, ribbon weaving; Fig. 19h, ribbon loom drawing

McBryde 1947, pl. 40c, ribbon weaving

Start 1948, p. 48, pl. VA, ribbon weaving; pl. VIB, belt weaving

Anderson 1978, p. 13, Fig. 3, pp. 142-44, Figs. 165-167, belt weaving; p. 66, Fig. 72, pp. 167-70, Figs. 188-189, ribbon weaving; p. 67, Fig. 74, pp. 166-67, Figs. 183-187, draw loom weaving

Textiles:

Maudslay 1899, color plate no. 1 bottom, huipil fabric (watercolor)

Osborne 1935, pp. 46-48, Fig. 10a-c, belt; pl. II, no. 7, hair ribbon

Breuer 1942, p. 13, huipil fabric

O'Neale 1945, Figs. 95a-c, 96a-c, 97a, huipils; Fig. 118j, k, hair ribbons; Figs. 119a-d, 120a, n, belts; Fig. 115f, servilleta; Figs. 125, 128, sarapes (Eisen); Fig. 122l, man's belt

Atwater 1954, frontispiece, ribbon (color); p. 207, no. 26, belt (color)

Atwater 1965, pl. IVc, belt

Anderson 1978, p. 169, Fig. 189, hair ribbons (details); p. 152, center left (color) draw loom textile; p. 150, lower right (color), belts; p. 149, upper right, embroidered square collars (color); p. 164, Fig. 183, draw loom huipil fabric

Color Renderings:

Osborne 1965, pl. 69, woman and man's cofradía (black and white), 1975, p. 251 (color)

Wood and Osborne 1966, pl. 50, woman

Petterson 1977, pp. 68-69, no. 12, woman; pp. 70-71, no. 13, man's cofradía

Text:

O'Neale 1945, pp. 192-93, 215-16, Eisen men's cofradía costumes; pp. 303-04, everyday costumes

Osborne 1965, pp. 148-50 (1975, pp. 212, 217-18), costumes

Drawings:

Osborne 1935, Fig. 10d, belt loom; 1965, pl. 65 (1975, p. 66), same belt loom

O'Neale 1945, Fig. 50e, g, h, hair ribbons; Figs. 50f, 51, 68k, belts; Figs. 24a, 26f, 34, 42a, huipils; Figs. 71a, l, 72c, m, 73ss, 68e brocaded motifs; Fig. 48a, d, women's wrap, weft ikat designs; Fig. 52b, plaid skirt fabric made in Salcajá

Fig. 90 Totonicapán belt, collected by Lilly de Jongh Osborne (354). Cotton and wool. 84 x 2¾" (2.14 m. x 7 cm.).

CHAPTER EIGHT
Quezaltenango

Quezaltenango is the second largest city in Guatemala as well as a departmental capital. In 1948, it had 49,000 inhabitants, of which 55 per cent were Quiché and the rest Ladino. The Quiché women still retain a distinctive costume, although it shows heavy European influence.

Several kinds of huipils, all woven on treadle looms, are worn. The richest type of huipil is shown in Color Plate II. It is made of three relatively narrow widths of fabric sewn together with a randa. Below the decorated area is a considerable length of white fabric, which is not visible when the huipil is being worn, as is the case in Fig. 96. The upper part has supplementary-weft patterning in purple cotton and yellow and magenta silk. The weft simply floats on the front to form the design, and between pattern areas on the back. The designs repeat in horizontal rows but the colors change across the row, giving the impression of greater complexity than is actually the case. Most of the motifs are probably not of native origin but are closely similar to designs found on European country textiles.[1] Similar huipils are still worn, but the randas in the newer examples have lavish floral decorations.[2]

The illustration in Fig. 92 shows the use of a ceremonial huipil of the type shown in Figs. 93 and 94. It is worn over the head instead of down on the shoulders. Often popularly referred to as a wedding huipil, it is also used for cofradía. The one shown in Fig. 93 is a spectacular (and probably late) example of a style that was in active use well before the Thirties and probably can be ascribed to the 19th century.[3] It is decorated with monochrome weft stripes, white on white, alternating heavier and finer wefts, and by random lengths of purple or yellow silk laid into the plain weave sheds.[4] The heavier wefts are longer than the others and create a rippled texture. The contrasting stripes across the center are done in purple, magenta and yellow, and the randas in purple. The beauty of the overall effect is unfortunately not conveyed by a black and white photograph.

The relationship of this huipil to the much more common twentieth century type seen in Fig. 94 is mainly in the layout.[5] They are both of three widths of fabric, with randas, with purple and yellow cross-stripes in the center and with floral embroidered neckbands. However, the later huipil has a more elaborate randa, with plant forms worked in but-

tonhole stitch, and is woven with a totally different technique. The fabric is actually produced on treadle looms in Totonicapán.[6] It has supplementary-weft patterning in both white and colored yarns (again, purple and yellow). Different examples have different proportions of white and colored patterning. The interlacing order is similar for both the white and colored wefts, but the colored wefts are discontinuous and turn at the edges of the motifs whereas the white supplementary wefts are woven passing from selvedge to selvedge, with long floats over the areas between motifs which are cut off only after the fabric has been woven. The ground is an open plain weave, so even interlacing the supplementary wefts 1/1, as is done in some parts of the designs, does not obscure them. Elsewhere they are interlaced 5/1/1/1, with the 5-span floats either in vertical alignment, or aligned in alternate pairs.[8] Supplementary wefts are inserted after alternate ground wefts.

A much more common type of everyday huipil than the one in Color Plate II is shown in Figs. 95-97. These are also woven in Totonicapán and bear some relationship to the huipils worn there, although the greatest similarities are found in older examples. There is horizontal banding of plain and patterned areas with the plain bands woven weft-faced in 3/1 twill or 3/1 broken twill. The Quezaltenango huipils are made of three widths rather than of two or one, however, and contain also some stripes with simple weft ikat patterning. The supplementary-weft patterning of the examples in Figs. 95 and 97 is done with a different technique than was the case for the huipil in Fig. 87. The supplementary wefts interlace 2/2, with each weft inserted opposite to the last so that when one weft is on the front, the next is on the back in the same place, creating a double-faced fabric. As with the first type of huipil discussed, the chief difference between the older and newer examples is in the randas, which are plain in Fig. 95 and floral in Figs. 96-97. The newer huipils usually also have a square instead of round neck opening.

The skirts of Quezaltenango differ from the others presented here in being gathered instead of wrapped. This is a definite European influence. A casing is sewn on the edge of the fabric and a drawstring is put through (see Fig. 98). In the example shown, the amount of fabric used is the maximum that would fit

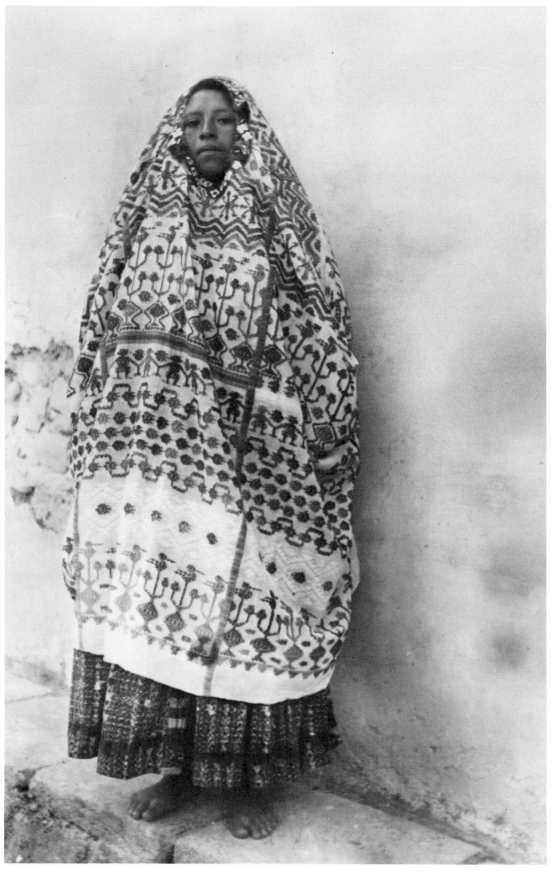

Fig. 92 Quezaltenango woman in ceremonial costume with veil, 1935. Middle American Research Institute, Tulane University, Matilda Geddings Gray Collection.

Fig. 93 Quezaltenango huipil used as veil, collected by Elsie
McDougall in 1940. Cotton and silk. 41 x 39″ (1.04 x .99 m.).
American Museum of Natural History 65/5298.

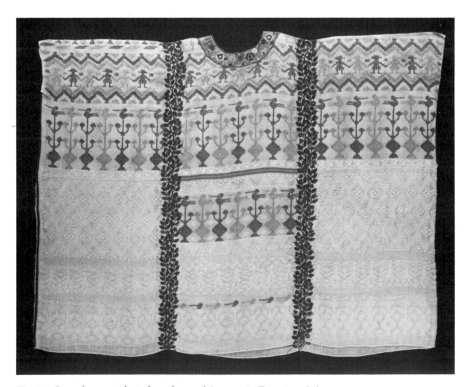

Fig. 94 Quezaltenango huipil used as veil (woven in Totonicapán),
collected by Lilly de Jongh Osborne (5), probably after 1930. Cotton
and silk. 38¼ x 49½″ (.97 x 1.26 m.).

Fig. 95 Quezaltenango huipil (woven in Totonicapán), collected by Lilly de Jongh Osborne (4), 1950. Cotton. 43 x 34¼" (1.09 x .87 m.).

in this manner around an average woman's waist (20′, 6.075 m.). The skirt in Fig. 98 is made of dark blue and white striped fabric of the same kind that is used in other villages. It has fine white weft stripes in groups of eight alternating with four pairs. The fabric is pieced with a horizontal randa that appears near the bottom of the skirt, and there are two vertical randas, one worn in front and the other in back. The many small creases are deliberately created by the storage method employed. The drawstring is pulled tight and the whole is twisted, as if to wring it, as far as it will go, -then folded in half and the drawstring wrapped around the hem to secure it. Also worn are similar skirts made of Salcajá-style double ikat fabric (Figs. 92 and 96). The exact pattern of use of the two types is not clear, but an ikat skirt is usually specified as being worn with the cofradía huipil as in Fig. 92. Apparently, either skirt can be worn with either of the regular huipils shown here.[9] The ikat skirts seem to be more common. The use of ikat skirts goes back at least to the turn of the century since there is an example in the Eisen collection.[10]

Although a drawstring secures the skirt, usually a narrow belt is worn as well. Some are plain red with a narrow black edge stripe on each side.[11] Others are black and white striped, of the type found in

many villages, but without any embellishment.[12] Still others are solid color with some brocaded motifs, as in Fig. 96.

For everyday wear, the most common hairstyle is with braids hanging down the back, sometimes with a strip of fabric braided in. For special occasions a very long Totonicapán ribbon may be worn (Fig. 99). The example in Fig. 99 is 28 yards long (25.6 m.). The ends of the ribbon have tapestry patterning in silk, and there are long tassels. The ribbon is wrapped around the head upon itself so that it stands out a considerable distance.[13]

The type of shawl commonly used in Quezaltenango is shown in Fig. 100. It is a single loom width with bold indigo warp ikat patterning and plain stripes in various colors; those shown in Fig. 100 are of purple, accented with narrow pale green silk. Other shawls have stronger colors such as hot pink and bright green solid stripes between the ikat. The knotting of the fringe into triangular points is typical. The original owner of the shawl had embroidered her initial on it.

A considerable variety of small and large cloths are made as servilletas or tablecloths. All are treadleloom woven. An example of a large tablecloth used for cofradía is shown in Fig. 101. It is two loom widths

Fig. 96 Quezaltenango woman, mid-Seventies. Photograph by
Marilyn Anderson.

Fig. 98 Quezaltenango skirt, collected by Lilly de Jongh Osborne (6), before 1960. Cotton. Length 29½"(75 cm.).

Fig. 97 Quezaltenango huipil (woven in Totonicapán), collected by Reuben Reina in 1970. Cotton. 40¼ x 42½" (1.025 x 1.08 m.). University Museum, University of Pennsylvania 70-13-58.

Fig. 99 Quezaltenango hair ribbon (woven in Totonicapán), collected by Lilly de Jongh Osborne (9), dating from before 1940. Cotton, wool, and silk; some metallic (tassels). 84' x 1¼" (25.6 m. x 3.5 cm.); tassels: 16" (40.6 cm.).

Fig. 101 Quezaltenango cofradía tablecloth, collected by Lilly de
Jongh Osborne (10). Cotton and silk. 71½ x 40¼″ (1.82 x 1.02 m.).

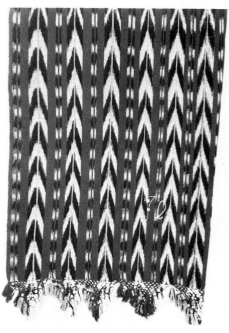

Fig. 100 Quezaltenango woman's shawl (detail), probably dating from before 1960. Cotton and silk. 86½" (including fringe) x 28¼" (2.20 x .72 m.). Collection of Fifi White.

sewn together, with fringed ends. It is of balanced plain weave with some weft stripes in red and some in heavier white yarn. It has supplementary-weft patterning in white cotton and in yellow and red silk. The supplementary weft floats on the front of the fabric to create the pattern and on the back between design areas, over multiples of two ground warps. The eight-pointed star designs are probably of European origin.

NOTES

1. See Pang 1977b for an introduction. The subject is one which should be pursued further.
2. Bunch 1977, p. 72.
3. Another example, though smaller and in well-worn condition is in the Museum of the American Indian, collected by Lothrop in the Twenties (16/615). It is of only two loom widths, as are a number of Quezaltenango daily huipils in the Eisen collection (O'Neale 1945, Figs. 91b and c, 92b). A third example, in the Tulane collection, is mentioned by O'Neale 1945, p. 129.
4. See also Bird 1953.
5. The huipil in Fig. 94 and the skirt in Fig. 98 are illustrated in color in Osborne 1965, pl. 43 (1975, p. 173). The side of the huipil shown is the opposite of the one in Fig. 94.
6. O'Neale 1945, p. 129; Osborne 1965, p. 156.
7. The Textile Museum has an example that has all-white supplementary wefts (1964.65.29). See also Anderson 1978, p. 145 right, which has only a little color. The example illustrated in Bird 1953, pl. V has mostly colored supplementary wefts, as does the one in Fig. 92 here.
8. The effect of 5/1/1/1 interlacing may be seen in the detail photograph that appears in Bird 1953, Pl. V below. In the section shown, the floats are in vertical alignment.
9. Ikat huipil with striped skirt combination mentioned by Osborne on her tag for a Quezaltenango belt (no. 20, red); huipil of type in Color Plate II with striped skirt: Muñoz and Ward 1940, p. 177, pl. 42; huipil of type in Color Plate II with ikat skirt: Osborne 1965, pl. 18a (1975, p. 128), Bunch 1977, p. 72.
10. O'Neale 1945, p. 164.
11. No. 20, dated 1958 and 3.5 cm. wide and No. 17, 2 cm. wide, in the Osborne collection. Also mentioned by O'Neale 1945, p. 293.
12. See Muñoz and Ward 1940, p. 177, pl. 42; O'Neale 1945, frontispiece e; Osborne 1965, pl. 18a (1975, p. 128); Kelsey and Osborne

1939/1961 plate opp. p. 120 (top).
13. See O'Neale 1945, frontispiece e.

REFERENCES
Ethnographic Photographs:
Kelsey and Osborne 1939, plate opp. p. 120 (top) men and women in cofradía dress
Muñoz and Ward 1940, p. 177, pl. 42 woman
Lemos 1941, p. 5 second from top, women
O'Neale 1945, frontispiece e, woman in fine huipil; 129b, woman in ikat huipil, skirt, and perraje
Bird 1953, pl. I, woman in ceremonial huipil
Osborne 1965, pl. 18a, b, women (1975, p. 128), b same as Lemos 1941, p. 5
Bunch 1977, p. 72, woman in fine brocaded huipil
Anderson 1978, p. 8, top center, woman in weft ikat huipil
Textiles:
Osborne 1935, pl. I, upper right, huipil fabric; pl. II, no. 4, huipil, no. 3, ikat huipil (color)
O'Neale 1945, Fig. 91a-c, draw loom huipils; Fig. 92b, huipil with ikat; Fig. 118f, g, hair ribbons
Bird 1953, pl. II, same as Fig. 93; pl. V, ceremonial huipil
Atwater 1965, pl. IIa, huipil with ikat
Osborne 1965, pl. 12a, detail of ikat huipil (1975, p. 84); pl. 43, two models, with and without veil (1975, p. 173)
Delgado 1968b, Fig. 10, p. 456, cofradía servilleta
Altman 1975, pl. 5 (color), ikat huipil
Tulane 1976, 17b, skirt; 17c, huipil (color)
Anderson 1978, p. 145 right (color), cofradía veil; p. 180, Fig. 204 center, neckline of ikat huipil
Heard 1979, pl. 12 left (color), unusual ikat shawl
Color Renderings:
Osborne 1965, pl. 31a, painting of wedding (black and white) (1975, p. 215); pl. 74, old and new style women's costumes (black and white) (1975, p. 258, color); pl. 75, man and woman in ceremonial costume (black and white), 1975, p. 259 (color)
Petterson 1977, pp. 118-19, no. 21, woman
Drawings:
O'Neale 1945, Figs. 24c, 27a, c, h, 31a, b, huipils; Fig. 52b, c skirt; 48c, wrap; 72k, 73nn, oo, designs
Atwater 1946 and 1965, no. 19, p. 35, huipil
Text:
O'Neale 1945, pp. 60, 292-294
Delgado 1963, pp. 327-329, costume in 1957

CHAPTER NINE
San Martín Sacatepéquez

San Martín Sacatepéquez, sometimes called Chile Verde, is located 12 miles (19 km.) west of Quezaltenango and near the Santa María volcano, which erupted in 1902, devastating the village. In addition to the usual agricultural subsistence activity, it supplies the nearby coffee plantations with baskets for the harvest. The population in 1948 was 9,000. The women's costume is similar to that of several nearby towns, including San Juan Ostuncalco and Concepción Chiquirichapa, but the men's costume is unique.

In the Thirties, some huipils were of three loom widths in San Martín, but the two-piece huipils were more common and later became the only kind made (Fig. 103).[1] The two-piece huipils are woven on a single warp and later cut apart, so they have a selvedge on only one end and are hemmed on the other. The center seam is sewn, leaving a gap in the middle for a neck slot. In many pieces, especially older ones, the seam is sewn with a decorative zigzag stitch in purple thread, but other colors were sometimes used. The ground fabric is invariably red.

Huipils of the Thirties have supplementary-weft patterning in relatively narrow bands framed by twill-woven weft stripes (Fig. 103) or weft stripes with three-span floats in alternate alignment. Typically, there are several pattern bands near the top and one or two at the bottom of the huipil. The patterned bands are separated by bands of the red ground. The supplementary wefts are most frequently woven in very short floats in vertical alignment (Figs. 103 and 106, and Color Plate XV). The weaving is done with the aid of an extra shed rod, which controls alternate warps that pass over the main shed, rod forming three-span floats which are short on account of the warp-predominant ground.[2] The vertical alignment of the floats results from using this same extra shed rod for each passage of the supplementary weft. The weaver must still select with a pick-up stick the warps needed for the design from those controlled by the extra shed rod. The supplementary weft floats on the back between design areas. The supplementary wefts are added after alternate ground wefts so that they do not appear closely packed. The favorite brocading yarns are purple and aqua silk floss. Dark green or yellow-orange cotton may be used as well. The designs are simple zigzags and diamonds.

The twill bands require additional loom con-trols; 3/1 twill, with the weft-float face on the front, is woven with a weft color that contrasts with the red ground. Four different sheds are required for this twill. The extra shed rod used for supplementary-weft patterning opens one shed, and an extra heddle rod is added to control those warps over the main shed rod not controlled by the extra shed rod. The warps in the main heddle rod may be similarly controlled by putting two sticks instead of one through the heddle loops, so that the loops in front of the sticks can be raised independently of those in back and vice versa.[3] The alternate warps of those controlled by the main heddle rod may also be picked up each time with the aid of a pick-up stick.[4]

During the Forties a new type of supplementary-weft patterning began to be used, though twill or other float weave bands still might outline the design areas.[5] The new designs are woven on a closed shed and without loom controls. The weaver selects the warps needed with the aid of a pick-up stick or just with her fingers.[6] The length of the floats is determined by the character of the design. The supplementary weft floats on the back between design areas. Various diamond designs are most commonly employed and purple is the predominant color for the supplementary weft, often of cotton instead of silk.

At the same time these changes were occurring, the plain ground areas between the design bands were eliminated, so that the twill or other float weave bands merely separate one design band from another. Some huipils have several narrow patterned bands and some have only a single wide band on each side. In the Sixties, the dividing twill bands were eliminated and the whole upper part of the huipil became one design area (see Color Plate XII). In some huipils the designs change at wide intervals without a plain band between, and in others the same design continues throughout. Usually there is still a band of continuous wefts at the bottom of the pattern area. In some examples, this may still be a float weave, but in others supplementary wefts may be used; the three-span floats may be in diagonal or alternating alignment (as in the example in Color Plate XII).

The current fashion (see Fig. 104) is to use the same technique, weaving without loom controls, but to produce more figurative designs. These designs are similar to those which have been in use in the nearby

Fig. 102 San Martín Sacatepéquez woman, 1935. Middle American
Research Institute, Tulane University, Matilda Geddings Gray
Collection.

towns of San Mateo and Concepción Chiquirichapa since the Thirties.[7] These potted plants and birds have a European character and their original source is probably Quezaltenango (see Color Plate II, for example), where there was a heavy European influence earlier. The designs appear in rows, but without twill or other contrast stripes between them. Different colors are used for adjoining sections of the designs, as occurs both in earlier San Martín huipils and on Quezaltenango huipils.[8]

The huipil is worn tucked into the skirt. The skirt is made of two lengths of dark blue treadle-loom woven fabric, each 22″ (56 cm.) wide and 7′4″ (2.24 m.) long (in Fig. 105), with a narrow zigzagging stitch in colored yarns side-to-side and into a tube. The fabric has lighter blue warp and weft stripes, a group of four narrow stripes alternating with two single stripes at even intervals. The warp stripes are much more closely spaced than the weft stripes. The woman steps into the tube, folds the top part down inside, and draws all extra fullness to the left side.[9]

The skirt is secured with a wide belt (Fig. 106 top) of black wool with white warp stripes, and corded fringe on the ends. The belt is spread out flat as it is wound around the waist. The ends are tucked under to secure it. The identical skirt and belt are worn in nearby towns such as Ostuncalco and Concepción Chiquirichapa. An apron of ikat fabric is commonly worn over the skirt (Fig. 104).

Today, the hair is simply braided with strips of commercial fabric and bound to the head, but formerly a handwoven ribbon was sometimes used (Fig. 107). The example illustrated is shorter than some that have been reported, although the reason is not clear.[10] The technique and designs with which it is woven are the same as for the earlier huipils, only without twill framing bands and with a dark blue instead of a red ground.

The woman's shawl is a large rectangle made of a single width of fabric and fringed on both ends (Fig. 108). In both Figs. 102 and 108 the heading strip has been left but in other examples, such as the one in Fig. 104, the heading strips are cut off. Like the hair ribbon, it has a dark blue ground. There are three groups of narrow red warp stripes dividing the width into fourths. There is usually a deep supplementary-weft patterned border at each end and small brocaded motifs scattered over the rest of the piece. Those on the example from the Thirties in Fig. 102 are simple geometric motifs but are not woven with the floats in vertical alignment as in the huipil. The floats are short, but are aligned according to the design, forming linear zigzags or diamonds, distinct from the later large diamond designs. There may in fact be longer floats on

Fig. 103 San Martín Sacatepéquez huipil, collected by Howard H. Tewksbury in the late Thirties. Cotton and silk. 29¼ x 34½″ (74 x 90 cm.). University Museum, University of Pennsylvania 66-34-74.

Fig. 104 San Martín Sacatepéquez man and woman, mid-Seventies. Photograph by Marilyn Anderson.

Fig. 107 San Martín Sacatepéquez hair ribbon, collected by Bernard J. Edley before 1953. Cotton and silk. 64¼ x 2¾″ (1.64 m. x 7 cm.). American Museum of Natural History 65-5337.

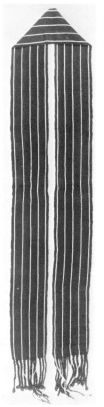

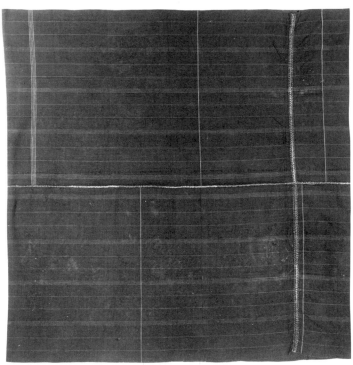

Fig. 105-106 San Martín Sacatepéquez skirt and woman's belt, collected by Lilly de Jongh Osborne (306, 312). Skirt: Cotton. 44 x 44″ (112 x 112 cm.). Belt: wool and cotton. 97 x 4½″ (2.46 m. x 11.5 cm.).

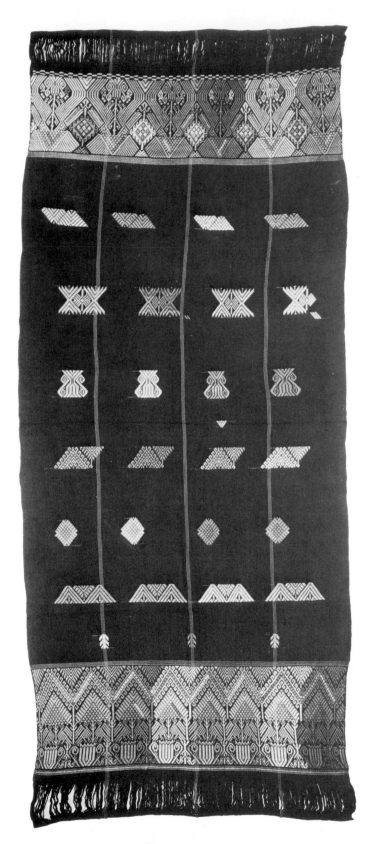

Fig. 108 San Martín Sacatepéquez woman's shawl, collected by Lilly de Jongh Osborne (313), probably after 1960. Cotton. 70 x 28¾" (1.78 x .73 m.).

Fig. 109 San Martín Sacatepéquez man: a, front; b, back, 1935. Middle American Research Institute, Tulane University, Matilda Geddings Gray Collection.

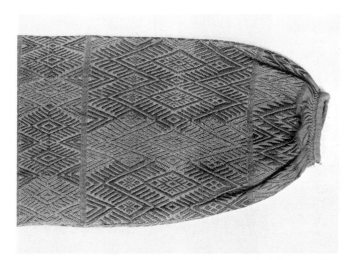

Fig. 110 San Martín Sacatepéquez man's shirt (detail of sleeve), collected by Lilly de Jongh Osborne (307), probably 1950-65. Cotton. 13½ x 8" (34 x 20.5 cm.) (sleeve only).

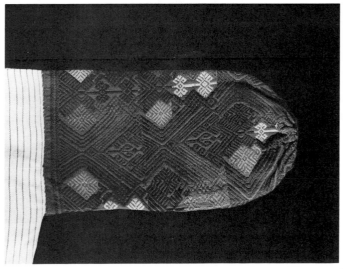

Fig. 111 San Martín Sacatepéquez man's shirt (detail of sleeve), collected by S.J. Muirden, 1967-75. Cotton. 46¾ x 26¾" (1.19 x .68 m.) (whole shirt). American Museum of Natural History 65/5901.

the back than on the front of the fabric. The exact date of the example in Fig. 108 is uncertain though it may well be from the Sixties. It has large diamond designs such as are found in huipils of this later period, and some of the bird and vase designs found on newer pieces as well. The newer shawls have wider borders than those on older ones. The newer examples may have warp stripes in green or purple instead of red; those in Fig. 108 are green.

The man's costume is one of the most spectacular in Guatemala (Figs. 104 and 109). It consists of a handwoven cotton shirt, pants, and sash, originally supplemented by a long capixay and large tzute. These latter items are not often used today. The shirt and pants are white with narrow red stripes. The shirt has a finished edge in front and fringe in back like a capixay, and it hangs to about knee length. The sleeves (Color Plate XV and Figs. 110 and 111) are red with supplementary-weft patterning, much like the huipil and following much the same stylistic development as can be seen by comparing the three examples illustrated.[11]

Examples from the Thirties usually have three patterned bands but some have as many as eight.[12] The bands may be outlined with supplementary-weft stripes instead of twill. The designs may be woven with three-span floats in vertical alignment as is usual for huipils or with the type of linear diamond and zigzag designs also found on the shawls. Both types of patterns may appear on the same piece. In the Forties the change to the larger type of diamond designs occurs and the red space between the bands is eliminated. In the Seventies, the horizontal banding is eliminated, and bird and plant designs are found.

The pants have a drawstring waist and come to about mid-calf length. They are patterned with supplementary wefts at the lower edge. In examples from the Thirties, the patterning is in purple silk and forms a narrow band of the linear-style diamond or zigzag patterns (barely visible in Fig. 109). Later examples, such as Fig. 112, have a slightly wider patterned band, with a larger type of diamond patterning, usually in cotton rather than silk. Recent examples, such as Fig. 104, may include additional colors besides the purple.

The sashes are very long with short corded fringes, have a red ground, are patterned in much the same way as the shirt sleeves (compare Figs. 109b and 113), and follow a similar sequence of technique and design changes. The example in Fig. 113, probably dating to the Fifties, has the ends patterned in the larger style of diamond design, and three bands across the center done with the older technique of floats in vertical alignment. The sash is worn wrapped around the waist twice, starting with the center in back, and

Fig. 112 San Martín Sacatepéquez man's pants, collected by Lilly de Jongh Osborne (306), probably 1950-65. Cotton. 29½ x 28¼" (75 x 72 cm.).

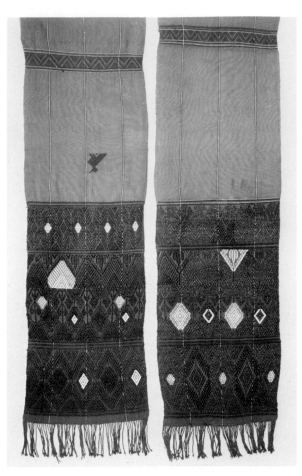

Fig. 113 San Martín Sacatepéquez man's sash (detail), collected by Lilly de Jongh Osborne (308), probably 1950-65. Cotton and silk. 13'8" x 12½" (4.17 x .315 m.).

finishing with the ends in back, where they are tied. The ends hang down (Fig. 109b). The sash is worn in this same way either over the capixay, or over the shirt if a capixay is not worn.

The capixay is made from heavy black wool. The sides are not sewn but as it is worn, the front overlaps the back panel. The front panel is hemmed, and the back panel has fringe and hangs down longer. The sleeves are sewn only for the last six inches or so. They are not worn on the arms but are folded back onto the wearer's back (see Fig. 109b). The photograph (Fig. 114) actually shows the capixay inside out; that is, the fringe on the shoulders is underneath the sleeve as the garment is being put on, and is exposed only when the wearer throws the sleeves onto his back.

The man's tzute is a large rectangle made of two loom widths (Fig. 115) with fringe at both ends or with a selvedge at one end and fringe at the other. The seam is sewn with a zigzag stitch of contrasting color,

and similar stitching is used to secure the fringed ends. It is red and there is a series of white (or orange and white) stripes down the middle of each width. In the Thirties, the wearing of very large tzutes was for the most part a thing of the past and younger men were wearing a smaller tzute or else a commercial bandanna.[13] Today, when the tzute is worn, which is not often, it may be a plain fabric, and not a bandanna (Fig. 104). To put it on, it is folded diagonally with the fold on the forehead and tied behind as seen in Fig. 109b.

NOTES
1. See Wood and Osborne 1966, pl. 44. Three-breadth huipils are also mentioned by O'Neale 1945, p. 277.
2. O'Neale 1945, pp. 64, 67.
3. O'Neale 1945, pp. 35, 71; Sperlich 1980, pp. 108-10 (Concepción Chiquirichapa).
4. Described by Delgado 1963, pp. 52-53.
5. Lemos 1941, p. 24 shows these designs in early form. A huipil (65/5335) and two men's sashes (65/5342c and 65/5343c) col-

Fig. 115 San Martín Sacatepéquez man's tzute, collected by Lilly de Jongh Osborne (310). Cotton. 56¼ x 47¼" (1.43 x 1.20) with fringe.

Fig. 114 San Martín Sacatepéquez capixay, collected by Lilly de Jongh Osborne (315), 1969. Wool. 57 x 86" (1.45 x 2.18 m.).

lected in 1953 by Bernard Edley and now at the American Museum of Natural History have most of their designs in the new style. The huipil has only one band near the lower edge with the older style of patterning.

6. See Anderson 1978, pp. 118-23, and Sperlich 1980, pp. 106-07, 137-38.
7. See, for example, O'Neale 1945, Fig. 111. The servilleta in (a) has some bands also in the technique with floats in vertical alignment. It appears that the same transition took place in Concepción, but at an earlier date. There is a huipil in the Eisen Collection from Concepción that is entirely patterned with three-span floats in vertical alignment, in bands framed by twill stripes (3-19).
8. See Sperlich 1980, pp. 64-65, for color photographs of San Martín women in these new huipils.
9. See O'Neale 1945, p. 277.
10. The examples cited by O'Neale 1945, pp. 276-77, are 96" long.
11. The shirt in Fig. 110 and the sash in Fig. 113 are illustrated in color in Osborne 1965, pl. 48 (1975, p. 181). Fig. 109a has been previously published in Handbook 1967, vol. 6, p. 151, Fig. 12.
12. The example with eight is in the Peabody Museum, 32-37/170, (collected 1932).
13. O'Neale 1945, p. 276. She describes the large older tzutes as hanging down to the calf of the leg. The examples in the Gray and Palmer collections are 69 x 66" (1.75 x 1.68 m.) and 69 x 56" (1.75 x 1.42 m.) slightly larger than Fig. 115.

REFERENCES
Ethnographic Photographs:
Osborne 1935, p. 92, Fig. 19, man (head only)
Kelsey and Osborne 1939, plate opp. p. 121 top, man playing flute
Mūnoz and Ward 1940, pl. 56, man
Lemos 1941, p. 24 lower right, man and woman
O'Neale 1945, Fig. 130d men
McBryde 1947, pl. 39c, three men and woman; pl. 41e left, man and woman
Lehmann 1961, p. 25, Fig. 18, boy
Osborne 1965, pl. 24c (1975, p. 156), men (traders); pl. 30b (1975, p. 214), man; pl. 34b (1975, p. 276), boys; pl. 38a (1975, p. 314), same photo as McBryde 1947, pl. 41e
Bunzl 1966, pp. 88-89, boy
Handbook 1967, vol. 6, p. 151, Fig. 12a, man (Tulane photo); p. 182, Fig. 28a, man playing flute
Marks 1976, Fig. 2, man—front and back (color)
Bunch 1977, p. 42, man (color)
Reina and Hill 1978, p. 232, pl. 396, man at shrine
Sperlich 1980, p. 64, woman; p. 65, women and girls (color); p. 69 top and bottom, women weaving (color)
Techniques:
O'Neale 1945, pp. 35, 64, 67, 71, Fig. 19f
Delgado 1963, pp. 52-53, Fig. 2
Anderson 1978, pp. 118-23, Figs. 136-140; p. 147 bottom, loom (color)
Sperlich 1980, pp. 106-107, 137-138
Textiles:
Lemos 1941, p. 24 top, huipil and shirt sleeves
Osborne 1965, pl. 48 (1975, p. 181), man's costume on model (color)
Heard 1979, p. 36, Fig. 5 top, huipil fabric; p. 49, Fig. 14 right, men's pants; p. 68, no. 3, man's costume on model (color)
Sperlich 1980, p. 137, pls. 63, 64, huipil
Color Renderings:
Crocker 1952, pl. 3
Wood and Osborne 1966, pl. 43, man; pl. 44, woman
Petterson 1977, pp. 216-17, no. 46, man and woman
Drawings:
O'Neale 1945, Fig. 45b, woman's shawl; Fig. 46b, c, woman's shawl; Fig. 47h, woman's shawl; Fig. 54r, capixay; Fig. 55e, pants
Text:
O'Neale 1945, pp. 276-77
Delgado 1963, pp. 329-31, 1957 costume

CHAPTER TEN

Todos Santos Cuchumatán

Of the many Mam villages in the Department of Huehuetenango that have fine handwoven costumes, only Todos Santos is mentioned in the literature before 1970 and only Todos Santos textiles are found in collections made before 1970. This puzzling circumstance appears to be due to the fact that the people of Todos Santos, especially the men, do a lot of traveling, mostly for trading purposes, and are often seen in other markets.[1] The red and white striped costume is indeed striking so it is no surprise that it should have been noticed. The village had a population of nearly 8,000 in 1948.

There are Todos Santos textiles from the turn of the century in both the Eisen collection and at the Smithsonian, collected by E. W. Nelson in 1899. O'Neale has published the Eisen huipil[2] and the Smithsonian's is shown in Fig. 116. They are of three loom panels sewn together without a randa. In Fig. 116 the side panels are somewhat longer than the center one, but this does not appear to be typical. The fabric is white with red warp stripes. In the Eisen huipil the red stripes are narrower than in the Smithsonian piece. The center panel is decorated with two broad, red, weft-faced stripes framed by fine green and yellow lines. The Eisen huipil has some weft-faced bands also in the side panels and a small amount of discontinuous-weft decoration in the form of small rectangles. These differences are within a range of variation comparable to that found among later pieces and do not necessarily reflect a difference in age between the two specimens.

The round neck hole is framed by a large ruffle of commercial fabric held down at the shoulders and front and back by small applied notched circles. The Eisen huipil has a slightly less full ruffle and, in addition, an applied silk braid which zigzags over it, a feature elaborated upon in later pieces, as can be seen in Fig. 118.[3] Wool braid or rickrack is used for this purpose in most later examples. The absence of applied braid makes the Smithsonian huipil more conservative, and probably older than the Eisen example.

The huipils of the Thirties and Forties seem to be nearly identical to the turn of the century pieces, although the available photographs, including Fig. 117, are not as clear as one might wish.[4] The huipil in Fig. 118 has patterning comparable to that of the Thirties and Forties but the size of the red stripes seems to be more typical of relatively recent pieces (compare Color Plate VII).

Sometime between 1950 and 1965, Todos Santos women began adding designs other than simple rectangles to their huipils (see Color Plate VII).[5] The colored threads that form these designs are supplementary to the red wefts.[6] Sometimes they are merely interlaced parallel to the red wefts, but linear designs (usually diagonals) are done by wrapping. A more recent technical innovation in Todos Santos huipils, apparently begun in the early Seventies, is weaving the weft-faced bands with discontinuous wefts of different colors as in tapestry weave, without the red ground. In the huipil shown in Fig. 119, the diamond designs are made with supplementary wefts, while the triangle designs are made of discontinuous wefts without the red ground.

The tendency to increase the size of the red warp stripes and decrease the white stripes has been another continuing change. And, although contemporary huipils vary somewhat from one another in this respect, there has been a general trend to increasing the amount of decoration on the huipil. Some recent huipils are entirely covered with polychrome weft patterning (see illustration p. 19). The type of yarns used has also changed. Although the red weft bands are usually woven of cotton, the brocaded motifs were often done with wool. Today acrylic is the most frequently used material. Another feature of many recent huipils is squared off neck ruffle corners, as seen in Fig. 119 and Color Plate VII. The round ones are smaller than in earlier examples.

The woman's skirt has not changed during the period of study. It is of dark blue cotton treadle-loom woven fabric, which has pairs of light blue weft stripes at intervals (Fig. 120). The width of the fabric (i.e., the length of the skirt) is 31" (79 cm.); this is increased by adding a strip about 3½" (9 cm.) wide to one side. The length of 10'4" (3.15 m.) is sewn into a tube. All the stitching is done by machine. The added strip may be worn either at the top or the bottom. The skirt is put on with folds toward the front from both sides (Figs. 117 and 119). One fold is a small tuck and the other is the entire end of the tube brought around from the back. The length of the skirt may vary with marital status,[7] from mid-calf to slightly above ankle length.

The belt, also shown in Fig. 120, is little

Fig. 117 Todos Santos woman and man, 1935. Middle American Research Institute, Tulane University, Matilda Geddings Gray Collection.

Fig. 116 Todos Santos huipil, collected by E.W. Nelson in 1899. Cotton. 34⅛ x 39″ (87 x 99 cm.). Department of Anthropology, Smithsonian Institution 201 089. Photograph by the author; black and white from color original.

changed. It is principally of red wool with fine black and white warp stripes. It is woven in warp-faced plain weave. The ends are braided and tie cords are attached. The belt is wound smoothly around the top of the skirt several times.

O'Neale describes a hair style made with a long wool ribbon, woven with red squares on a yellow ground.[8] Each half of the ribbon is wound around a hank of half the woman's hair and the two ends are tied in a bow on top of the head. A ribbon in the Osborne collection at the University Museum, Philadelphia, would serve the same purpose (42-35-421). It is simply warp-predominant plain weave with heavy red wool warps (and side edges with blue cotton warps) and thin dark blue cotton wefts. It appears from recent photographs that this hair style is not used any longer. The most common style is simply to braid the hair in two plaits down the back, sometimes working in a ribbon of commercial fabric. Todos Santos is one of the few towns where the women commonly wear hats, in this case straw hats.

O'Neale describes the local handwoven woman's tzute as a large square with dark red or brown ground striped with several wide units made up of fine white stripes.[9] This tzute was not often collected and as early as the Thirties was being replaced either by a square of skirt fabric (see Fig. 117) or by a commercial bandanna. The tzute was worn draped over the back with two corners tied across the chest, as in Fig. 117. By the Fifties, commercial yardage or silk scarves were being used, and today commercial yardage is the usual material.[10]

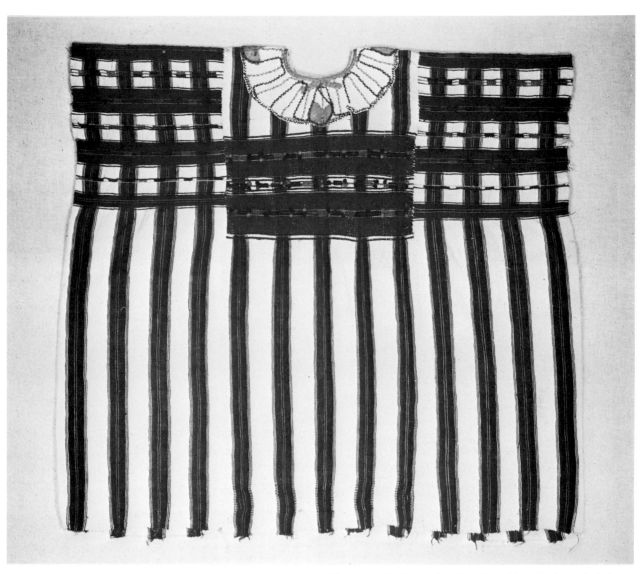

Fig. 118 Todos Santos huipil, collected by Lilly de Jongh Osborne (242), before 1965. Cotton and wool. 34¼ x 34¼" (87 x 87 cm.).

The man's costume consists of cotton shirt and pants, and wool overpants and some type of jacket. The late 19th century costume is shown in Fig. 121. As with the woman's costume, there are examples available in early collections. Interestingly enough, both the shirt in the Eisen collection and one in the Smithsonian are made of commercial muslin fabric with only the collar and cuffs handwoven.[11] The cuffs are only about ½" (1.3 cm.) wide and so, though decorated, are not prominent. The collar is usually white with red weft-faced bands, similar to the huipil. Shirts of the Thirties and Forties, as shown in Fig. 123, are entirely handwoven, and have narrow warp stripes in brown, blue, red or yellow on a white ground.[12] There is a concentration of stripes in the center front and back. The sleeves may be cut with the

stripes either lengthwise or crosswise. New shirts have more stripes closer together in more different colors, and heavily decorated collars and cuffs, similar to the huipil (Figs. 124 and 125). The snap-front closure and patch pocket of the shirt in Fig. 125 is a very recent innovation and is not yet universally used.

The pants are ankle length, and also made of backstrap-loom woven fabric. In the late nineteenth century examples shown in Fig. 121, the red warp stripes are relatively narrow and far apart. The man in the center has no visible warp stripes on his pants. All have some broad weft-faced bands at intervals. Both in the Thirties and Forties there were pants very similar to these nineteenth century ones, with weft-faced bands similar to the contemporary huipils (Fig. 126, see also Fig. 117), and pants with much broader

Fig. 119 Todos Santos woman with her daughter, 1979. Photograph by Emily Norton; black and white from color original.

Fig. 120 Todos Santos skirt and woman's belt, collected by Lilly de Jongh Osborne (328, 237). Skirt: cotton. 29¼ x 27½″ (74 x 70 cm.). Belt: wool. 54¼ x 3⅛″ (138 x 8 cm.).

red warp stripes and no weft-faced bands (Fig. 122). The most frequently seen style of pants today is descended from this second type (Fig. 125), with the red stripes even broader than the white ones. Occasionally, pants with weft-faced bands similar to those on the newer huipils are found.

An example of a man's sash is shown in Fig. 127. It is a four-selvedge rectangle with both warp and weft stripes in red and white. The red stripes are wider at the ends than in the center and the warps seem to be spread further apart in this area also. This sash represents a commonly used type from the Thirties and Forties, and probably later as well.[13] However, some sashes were fringed, and some had narrow green, blue or yellow as well as red and white stripes.[14] Although some modern sashes are red and white, some have polychrome warp stripes.[15] Some sashes also have wool pompons on the ends.[16]

Although the sash is shown tied at center front in the late nineteenth century photograph (Fig. 121), it is in later times usually tied over the left hip (as in Fig. 122), or sometimes the right hip. The knot usually has one loop and the ends hang down a short distance.[17] Sometimes the sash is clearly visible and sometimes it is hidden by the overpants.

The overpants are made from natural black wool, woven locally on treadle looms. The tailoring is relatively elaborate,[18] and not unlike that of the ceremonial overpants from other towns. In the late nineteenth century photograph, these overpants are the same length as the pants, while in the photographs from the Thirties, they are a few inches shorter, reaching about mid-calf level. In the Forties, they are slightly higher, coming near the top of the calf.[19] Today they are only about knee height and lack the buttonholes on the legs found in the older examples (Fig. 125).[20]

The wool jackets varied considerably, even within one given period. A black wool pullover jacket of local manufacture occurs in the late nineteenth century photograph as well as later.[21] The man in Fig. 117 has on a dark wool knee-length capixay, probably also of local make. A gray or blue and white striped wool jacket, open in front, was also worn. Examples from the Thirties and Forties often have a line of simple tapestry patterning around the lower edge (Figs. 122 and 128).[22] This type of jacket is from Sololá. Plain dark blue wool jackets, made in Momostenango, were also worn.[23] Today jackets are not regularly worn except in cold weather, when either a blue jacket or a capixay, similar to the older ones although not made locally, is worn.[24] Some small boys wear zipper-front jackets.[25]

Although young men have now virtually ceased wearing it (Fig. 125), a tzute was commonly worn on the head, usually under a straw hat. O'Neale describes the original handwoven tzute as red, although the examples shown in the early photograph seem to be white. By the Thirties a commercial bandanna was the usual substitute. It was worn differently than the tzutes already discussed. After being folded into a triangle, it was tied tightly around the head with the knot over the left ear (or sometimes the right ear). The corners of the cloth stick out but do not fall to the shoulders. The man in Fig. 122 is wearing a bandanna in this fashion, but it does not show very clearly.[26] Occasionally a second bandanna is worn tied around the neck; this may be a badge of office.[27]

NOTES
1. McBryde 1947, p. 50 and note 80.
2. O'Neale 1945, Fig. 103a.
3. The huipil in Fig. 118, and the man's shirt and sash (Figs. 123 and 127), along with other parts of the Todos Santos costumes in her collection, are illustrated in color in Osborne 1965, pl. 41.
4. See also O'Neale 1945, Fig. 130b, and Marden 1947, p. 533. Both women are shown in profile.
5. Osborne 1965, pl. 19a shows a woman with such a huipil. The red warp stripes on this piece are smaller and farther apart than the more conservatively patterned huipil in Fig. 118.
6. The structure of the weft-faced bands is too complex to describe in detail here, but it is adequately described in Sperlich 1980, pp. 111-18, 167-70.
7. Pancake 1976, p. 7.
8. O'Neale 1945, p. 70 and Fig. 23t. A single specimen in the Palmer collection was studied. The weave described is a plain-weave-derived float weave. I have not been able to examine a specimen myself. Although she says that the technique is identical to some Peruvian bands she had published earlier, this is not the case, since the bands in question are woven in plain weave with warp substitution. The issue is further clouded by some garbling of the reference, which should presumably be p. 189 (not p. 178), pl. 43a, c-e (not a-e, since b is woven in complementary-warp weave). The hair style is described in O'Neale 1945, p. 303. See Lemos 1941, p. 15 lower right for a photograph. The same style and ribbon seems to be depicted in Wood and Osborne 1966, pl. 55. Delgado (1963, p. 312) mentions a red wool ribbon.
9. O'Neale 1945, p. 303.
10. Delgado 1963, p. 312 for the Fifties; information on today from Emily Norton, personal communication.
11. Another example is in the Osborne collection in the University Museum, Philadelphia (42-35-422).
12. See Osborne 1965, pl. 41 for a color illustration of this piece.
13. A similar sash occurs in the Osborne collection at the University Museum (42-35-424). Sashes are shown being worn in photographs in Marden 1947, p. 533; Osborne 1965, pls. 25a (man second from right), 26a. See also Crocker 1952, pl. 6.
14. O'Neale 1945, p. 303 described fringed sashes in the Palmer and Gray collections. See also Wood and Osborne 1966, pl. 54 and p. 138. A sash in the Lamson-Scribner collection at the Textile Museum (1964.65.109) has the warp ends closely knotted for 3½" (9 cm.) with wool pompons at the ends.
15. See the color photograph in Sperlich 1980, p. 63. Also Delgado 1963, p. 313. The modern sash in the Heard Museum collection is mainly red and white (Heard 1979, pl. 9, p. 43 left).
16. O'Neale mentions wool pompons on the fringed sashes (see note 13). The Heard Museum sash has pompons without fringe (see note 15).

127

Fig. 121 Todos Santos men, late nineteenth century. Peabody
Museum, Harvard University. Photograph by George Byron Gordon.

Fig. 122 Todos Santos man, 1935. Middle American Research Institute, Tulane University, Matilda Geddings Gray Collection.

Fig. 123 Todos Santos man's shirt, collected by Lilly de Jongh Osborne (229), before 1965. Cotton and wool. 34½ (back) x 62¼"(sleeve end to sleeve end) (.87 x 1.58 m.).

Fig. 124 Todos Santos man's shirt, collected by Leonel Beteta in the Seventies. Cotton and acrylic. 31 x 27½" (79 x 69 cm.).

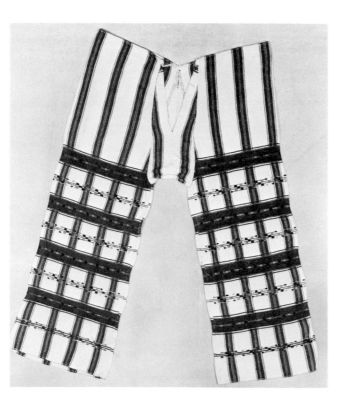

Fig. 126 Todos Santos man's pants, of style found in the Thirties and Forties. Cotton and wool. Length: 39″ (99 cm.). Ruth Jamison collection.

Fig. 125 Todos Santos man, 1979. Photograph by Emily Norton; black and white from color original.

Fig. 127 Todos Santos man's sash, collected by Lilly de Jongh Osborne (230) before 1965. Cotton. 7½' x 9½" (2.30 x .24 m.).

Fig. 128 Todos Santos man's jacket, collected by Lilly de Jongh Osborne (238), probably dating from the Thirties. Wool. 24 x 17¼" (61 x 44 cm.).

17. Shows most clearly in Osborne 1965, pl. 26a.
18. See diagram of cut in O'Neale 1945, Fig. 55g.
19. See Marden 1947, p. 533.
20. See also Anderson 1978, p. 8 lower left; Liebler 1980, p. 53.
21. See McBryde 1947, pl. 31a.
22. Marden 1947, p. 533 shows this jacket in color.
23. See Wood and Osborne 1966, pl. 54.
24. See Bunch 1977, pp. 64-65. Information also from Emily Norton.
25. See Sperlich 1980, p. 63 and cover of *Popular Photography*, Jan. 1974.
26. For clearer examples, see Muñoz and Ward 1940, p. 184, Fig. 45 (who seems to have a plain red tzute); Marden 1947, p. 532; Osborne 1965, pls. 25a, 26a (1975 pp. 157, 158).
27. See Marden 1947, p. 532, an alguacil, and Osborne 1965, pl. 25a, man second from left, who also has a fancy jacket, and sash crossed over his chest.

REFERENCES
Ethnographic Photographs:
La Farge 1931, p. 11, Fig. 2, men
Marden 1936, p. 437, pl. I, two photos, men (color)
Kelsey and Osborne 1939/61, 5th plate after p. 56, man
Muñoz and Ward 1940, p. 184, pl. 45, man
Lemos 1941, p. 3 right, man, same as Muñoz and Ward; p. 15, lower right, women
O'Neale 1945, Fig. 130b, man and woman
Marden 1947, p. 532, man (color); p. 533, men and woman (color)
McBryde 1947, pl. 31a (caption p. 172), man and boy
Osborne 1965, pl. 19a (1975, p. 129), woman; pl. 25a, b (1975, p. 157), men; pl. 26a (1975, p. 158), man
Handbook, vol. 7, 1969, p. 51, fig. 2, boys
Popular Photography Jan. 1974, cover, boy and girl (color)
Bjerregaard 1977, p. 11, man, woman and boy
Bunch 1977, pp. 64-65, two men and woman (color)
Anderson 1978, p. 8 lower left, man; p. 30, Fig. 17, couple; p. 33, Fig. 20, man
Heard 1979, p. 65 (below) woman weaving (color)
Sperlich 1980, pls. 1, 2, 3, beating cotton; p. 18, pl. 11, winding yarn; p. 21, pl. 14, warping; p. 62, woman spinning (color); p. 63, girl and two boys (color); p. 93, pl. 39, woman weaving; p. 118, pl. 48, woman weaving
Liebler 1980, p. 53, two men
Techniques:
O'Neale 1945, pp. 66-67, Figs. 19d, 23n, r, t, loom
Sperlich 1980, pp. 111-18, compound weave; pp. 167-70, huipil
Textiles:
O'Neale 1945, Fig. 103a, huipil (Eisen)
Osborne 1965, pl. 41, men's and women's costumes (color), 1975 p. 169
Anderson 1978, p. 184, Fig. 209 top, huipil neck
Heard Museum 1979, p. 43, Fig. 9 (right, underneath), sash (color); p. 49, Fig. 14 left, men's pants and overpants; p. 72 top, no. 4, 5, men's and women's costumes (color)
Sperlich 1980, p. 168, pls. 87, 88, huipil
Color Renderings:
Crocker 1952, pl. 6, men and woman
Osborne 1965, pl. 78 (1975, p. 262), man and woman
Wood and Osborne 1966, pl. 54, man; pl. 55, woman
Petterson 1977, pp. 230-31, no. 53, man and woman
Drawings:
O'Neale 1945, Fig. 54b, shirt (Eisen); Fig. 54c, black wool coat (Tulane); Fig. 24k, huipil construction; Fig. 55k, pants construction; Fig. 55g, overpants construction (Tulane)
Wood and Osborne 1966, p. 140, huipil neckline
Text:
O'Neale 1945, pp. 302-03, costume
Delgado 1963, pp. 312-13, costume in 1957
Background:
Oakes 1951a and b
Dutton 1939, All Saints' Day ceremonies

CHAPTER ELEVEN
Santa María Nebaj

Nebaj is the largest of the three Ixil villages, with a population of 15,000 in 1948. That number increased to more than 23,000 by 1964, of which only slightly over 5,000 lived in town. Nebaj is located in a mountainous area in the west of the department of El Quiché. Many of the men supplement their local agricultural work with seasonal labor on the coffee plantations of the Pacific lowlands.

A few pieces in early collections provide information on Nebaj textiles from the turn of the century. There are two types of three-panel huipils, corresponding to the later versions shown in Color Plate XI and Fig. 130. Both have plain white side panels, and a central section with red weft stripes. In one, the central section is sufficiently weft-faced for the red to be prominent, as in Fig. 130, and in the other, the fabric is warp-predominant so that the red does not show very much, as in Color Plate XI.[1] The supplementary-weft patterning is relatively simple, consisting of horizontal zigzags, triangles, some small birds, and a band of horizontal chevrons near the neckline, done primarily in green, yellow, yellow-orange, and red cotton. They have applied loops on the neckline as do the later examples.

The method of inserting the supplementary wefts differs from the later examples, however. In these early huipils, the supplementary wefts are laid in the same shed as the ground weft, or form only very short floats (in some, though not all, of the motifs in the warp-faced examples), which means that in the weft-faced examples they show much more clearly than in the warp-predominant ones.[2] In the latter case, some motifs are given additional definition by beginning the brocading with the center of the supplementary-weft yarn, and crossing the two ends in the shed each time. The turn of the wefts on the front of the fabric creates a small ridge on both sides of the design.

That both these types of huipil were regularly worn tucked into the skirt is suggested by the two photographs from the Forties shown here (Figs. 129 and 131).[3] The type with the weft-faced center is worn by the woman in Fig. 129, and the type with the warp-predominant center seems to be worn by her daughter, as well as by two women at center left in Fig. 131. The cofradía huipil, also shown in Fig. 131, seems to be very similar to the type with a weft-faced central section. The actual distinction is not clear, except that the cofradía huipil may be larger. It is of course worn

in the specifically cofradía manner, hanging loose over the regular clothing.

It is likely that the huipils in Color Plate XI and Fig. 130 were made at about the same time as the photographs. They are similar to their turn-of-the-century counterparts in over-all layout but differ in detail. The most interesting difference is that the supplementary wefts float on the front of the fabric instead of being laid in. On the warp-predominant example (Color Plate XI), the floats are 11-15 span, while on the weft-faced example (Fig. 130), most floats are three-span. In both types, the brocading wefts are often begun at the center and turn on the front, but the effect is not as dramatic as on the older examples. The two ends of the brocading wefts interlace identically, and since the yarn used is a silk floss or cotton composed of grouped singles, the two ends combine to produce the appearance of a single heavier yarn.

These later huipils also differ from the earlier ones in their much more extensive use of silk supplementary weft yarns, chiefly in two shades of purple, aqua, orange, and yellow. The range of colors used in the huipil in Fig. 130 is similar to the example shown in Color Plate XI, although the prominence of the red weft stripes reduces the purple effect found on the warp-predominant example. Some innovative motifs such as people, animals, and plants are found on these later huipils.

The cofradía huipil used today is very similar in over-all format to its counterpart of the Forties, although usually it is less finely woven and is brocaded with mercerized cotton rather than silk.[4] However, a third brocading technique is employed, different from both of the earlier ones.[5] The brocading thread is begun at the end rather than the middle so that there are no ridges on the edges of the motifs. The weft interlaces both right to left and left to right between each passage of the ground weft, each passage interlacing in alternate alignment to the first. The effect of parallel floats characteristic of the earlier technique is therefore lost.

This same type of supplementary-weft patterning is also found in the type of three-panel huipil now in daily use (see Fig. 132 left).[6] This huipil is clearly derived from the type represented by the cofradía huipil, the evidence including the fact that it has red wefts in the pattern bands (although these are usually almost completely covered up by the supplementary

132

Fig. 129 Nebaj family, 1942. Peabody Museum, Harvard University, Carnegie Institution Archives.

Fig. 130 Nebaj huipil, probably from the Thirties. Cotton and silk.
31½ x 48¾" (.80 x 1.24 m.). Collection of Ambassador William G.
Bowdler.

wefts). There are still sideways chevron bands on the shoulders and near the bottom are some white-ground bands with zigzags and triangles. But the principal pattern bands, instead of spaced figural motifs, have solid diamond and triangle designs.

Another type of everyday huipil also occurs in Nebaj (Figs. 133 and 134).[7] It is made of two panels of fabric, and the neck band has points instead of parallel edges. The motifs, mainly figural, are brocaded in unoutlined rows. The ground fabric is warp-faced and white. In the older of the two examples shown, the brocading technique matches that of the three-breadth huipils from the Thirties and Forties, while in the newer one it corresponds to that of the contemporary three-breadth huipils.[8] The motifs are also larger and closer together on the more recent examples.

The current literature indicates that the two-panel style, evidently common in the Sixties, has been substantially replaced by the three-panel style shown in Fig. 132 during the Seventies. There are transitional forms in which the two-panel huipil has horizontal supplementary-weft bands dividing the designs and in which the three-panel huipil has figural motifs.[10] The two-panel style was used at least as early as the Forties (see, for example, the child on the right in Fig. 131), and the scale of the decoration on huipils of this date is comparable to Fig. 133.[11]

A completely new type of huipil is now coming into use, unfortunately not handwoven (Fig. 132, right). The neck opening of this commercial fabric huipil is embellished with chain stitches sewn on by machine. The remainder of the costume is still traditional.

The skirt appears to have remained a constant during the period of study (Fig. 135). It is made of treadle-loom woven fabric, predominantly red in color, with narrow weft stripes in yellow and ikat yarns at spaced intervals. One complete loom width

Fig. 131 Nebaj women in cofradía and everyday costume, 1942.
Peabody Museum, Harvard University, Carnegie Institution Archives.

Fig. 132 Nebaj women, 1980. Photograph by Susan Masuoka.

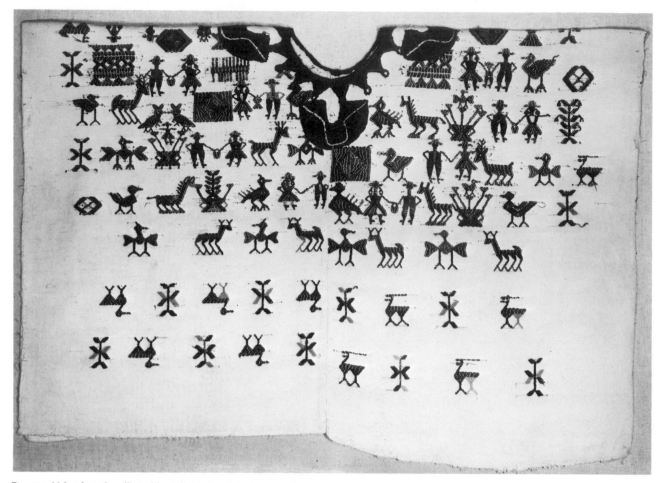

Fig. 133 Nebaj huipil, collected by Lilly de Jongh Osborne (191), probably dating from the Thirties or Forties. Cotton 27¾ x 41¾" (.705 x 1.06 m.).

Fig. 134 Nebaj huipil, collected by Fifi White in the Seventies (Sixties style). Cotton. 26 x 43¼" (66 x 110 cm.).

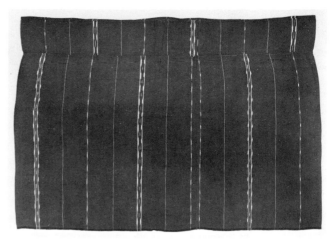

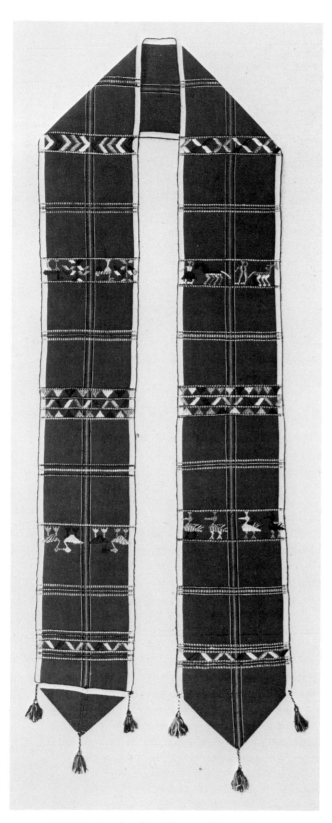

Fig. 135 Nebaj skirt, collected by Lilly de Jongh Osborne (219). Rayon. 42¼ x 59″ (1.07 x 1.50 m.).

Fig. 136 Nebaj hair band, collected by Matilda Geddings Gray, probably dating from the Thirties or Forties. Cotton and silk. 8′6″ x 7″ (2.60 x .18 m. excluding tassels). Middle American Research Institute, Tulane University G.4.3.10. Gift of Mrs. Harold H. Stream.

(36″, 91 cm.) and part of another (7″, 18 cm.) are sewn together, with the narrower piece worn either at the top or at the bottom. The length (9′10″, 3 m.) is sewn into a tube. All the stitching is done by machine. The skirt is wrapped snugly with the end passing around the back, ending on the left side. In the older photographs, it is usually shown worn to ankle length, but now it may sometimes be worn slightly shorter.

It is held in place by a belt (see Color Plate I), often elaborately patterned. An example collected by Gordon for the Peabody Museum in 1901 (01-40/C3027) is basically similar to the later examples shown, but lacks any patterning on the sides. The central portion is patterned mainly with horizontal stripes and with occasional small hourglass and larger diamond forms. Almost the entire length of the belt is decorated in this fashion. Red cotton, and dark pink, yellow, and green silk are used for the supplementary wefts. A feature which occurs on this example that all later ones seem to lack is that in areas where the white ground of the belt shows, as for example in the middle, and surrounding the hour glass and diamond designs, alternate warps are interlaced 3/1 with the three-span floats in alternating alignment (warp-faced alternating float weave). A slightly later belt, collected by Lothrop in 1917 (Peabody Museum, 17-3/C7779), is similar but lacks this float weave, and has plant motifs brocaded in the side panels on one end (in the Thirties technique). Again, red cotton is the dominant supplementary-weft color, although some silk, magenta instead of dark pink, is used. These two belts, although forming a very small sample, probably represent the general stylistic development during this time.

The examples shown in Color Plate I, probably

Fig. 137 Nebaj hair band (detail), collected by Lilly de Jongh Osborne (185), probably dating from the Sixties. Cotton. 11'6" x 13½" (3.5 x .34 m.).

Fig. 138 Nebaj hair band, collected by Ruth Jamison in 1978. Cotton. 10'4" x 21½" (3.15 x .55 m. excluding tassels).

from the Thirties, and c. 1970 respectively, are representative of these periods, although there are some modern belts that are patterned on both ends. The earlier example (on the left), has a higher weft count than the newer one on the right and is brocaded with silk instead of cotton. It also has smaller and less complex patterns. The central section of the belt is technically identical in all examples. The supplementary wefts are inserted in an open shed, over and under multiple warps, with the aid of supplementary shed rods.[12] The combination of passing the supplementary wefts over multiple warps, and inserting four or six of them for each ground weft, means that the patterned

area appears weft-faced, although the plain areas (including the back) of the belt are completely warp-faced. The motifs on the sides of the belt are brocaded similarly to the two-panel huipil, with most of the motifs in the earlier belt done in the technique described for huipils of the same period, and those in the later belt done in the more modern technique. The belt is worn wrapped around the waist several times, with the end tucked under.

The Nebaj woman's usual hairdress is one of the most grandiose in all of Guatemala (Fig. 132). A very broad, very long, locally woven band is used (Fig. 138) to bind up the hair. The example shown in

Fig. 139 Nebaj woman putting up her hair, 1973.
  a Twisting the band.
  b Winding the band around the hair at the nape of the neck.
  c Twisting the band on itself and then spirally around the hair.
  d The finished effect seen from the back. The two ends of the band have been tied together at the top of the head.
Photographs by Ambassador William G. Bowdler; black and white from color originals.

Fig. 136 is smaller than may have been usual, but gives an idea of what this hairband was like in the Thirties and Forties. It is predominantly red, with white warp stripes at the sides and some colored stripes in the center. It has a few brocaded motifs in silk, in the usual technique of the period. The ends are folded into a triangle and a small tassel is attached to each corner. Modern hair bands are like the example shown in Fig. 138, with multicolor stripes, red and green prominent among them, and usually without brocading. A width of 21″ (55 cm.) is typical. The example in Fig. 137, perhaps from the Sixties, seems to be transitional. It is 8″ (20 cm.) narrower, has broad red stripes in the center with colored stripes at the edges, and the

brocaded panel shown near one end. This brocading is done in the modern technique.

The manner of putting on the hairband is shown in Fig. 139. The woman demonstrating has her shawl, which should not be confused with the hair band, draped over her right shoulder. In (a) she twists one end of the band on itself (the other end is draped over her right arm). In (b) she has placed one end of the band over her right shoulder (the tassels start at about waist level). The hair and the remainder of the band are drawn over the left shoulder (that end still draped over her right arm). The band is twisted around the loose hair at the nape of the neck. In (c) the band, first twisted tightly on itself, is wound around the hair spirally from the nape of the neck to the ends. When the hair becomes thin, a cord is added to it so that the band can be wound beyond the length of the hair to make a roll of the desired length. The remaining end at the tip of the roll is now about the same length as the end on the right shoulder. She places the roll up over her forehead, and then down the right side, drawing the end up again toward the top on the left, and bringing the end from the right shoulder up toward the top on the right. She ties the two ends together just behind the roll above the forehead, and with her thumbs under the knot from behind, pushes it under and up slightly. The tassels of the band fall down the back of the head as shown in (d).[14]

The woman's shawl is shown in Figs. 140 and 141. It is made of two loom widths, and fringed at both ends. The seams in both examples shown are done by machine. The older example has predominantly red and black stripes with narrow white, green, and orange ones, and has a small amount of brocading in the Thirties and Forties technique.[15] The more recent one has multicolored stripes, with a considerable use of green, as well as black, red, and other colors. The decoration is of machine embroidery in white thread. Not all modern shawls have this much decoration. The shawl may be folded over the head as a sun shade or merely flung over one shoulder (see Figs. 131 and 139). It is also used for baby-carrying.[16]

Smaller tzutes are shown in Figs. 142 and 143.[17] They are single-width pieces with fringe on both ends. The stylistic development is similar to the other types of textiles covered. The older example is predominantly red and has motifs brocaded in silk, using the same technique as is found in huipils of the period. The newer example has a stripe layout very similar to the older one, but the red stripes are narrower. The ends next to the fringe are finished with machine stitching. The brocading is especially lavish. Some of it is done in the older technique and some in the newer. Its collection date of the mid-Sixties thus gives an indication of when the transition was taking place. Tzutes like that in Fig. 143 are worn by women for cofradía, folded on the head.[18]

NOTES

1. The sample includes two huipils in the Heyde Collection at the American Museum of Natural History, 65/2090 with a weft-faced central section (and some purple silk brocading in addition to the cotton), and 65/2089 with a warp-predominant central section. Another huipil of the latter type (all cotton) was acquired in 1918 by the Museum of the American Indian, 9/8185. Although it does not show in Fig. 130, the huipils with weft-faced center sections, both from the turn of the century and from the Thirties and Forties, have heavier wefts inserted at intervals in the white side sections, creating a ribbed effect.

2. This brocading differs technically from, and is far less rich than,

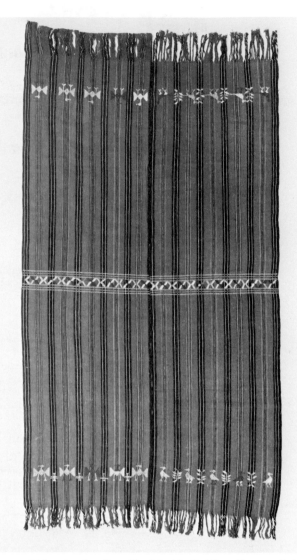

Fig. 140 Nebaj shawl, collected by Matilda Geddings Gray, probably dating from the Thirties or Forties. Cotton and silk. 76 x 38½" (1.93 x .98 m. including fringe). Middle American Research Institute, Tulane University G.4.3.9. Gift of Mrs. Harold H. Stream.

that on the man's sashes of the same period, familiar from O'Neale 1945, Fig. 123b, c. There are also two Ixil sashes in the Heyde Collection (AMNH 65/2094, 65/2098).

3. See also Marden 1945, pl. IX top, which shows two women in huipils with the warp-predominant center section; Wood and Osborne 1966, pl. 29.

4. Several recent illustrations of the cofradía huipil in use have been published: Colby and Berghe 1969, pl. 12; Ordoñez and Paz 1975, cover (color), p. 43; Bunch 1977, p. vi (color).

5. The modern cofradía huipil analyzed is the example in Ambassador William G. Bowdler's collection. The dimensions of this huipil are 33 x 51" (84 x 129 cm.).

6. See Sperlich 1980, pp. 134-36.

7. The huipil in Fig. 133 is published in color in Osborne 1965, pl. 42, 1975, p. 171. The opposite face of the huipil is shown from that illustrated here.

8. See Sperlich 1980, pp. 150-52 and Anderson 1978, pp. 91-92 for further technical details on recent examples.

9. Anderson 1978, p. 91; Ordoñez and Paz 1975, p. 48.

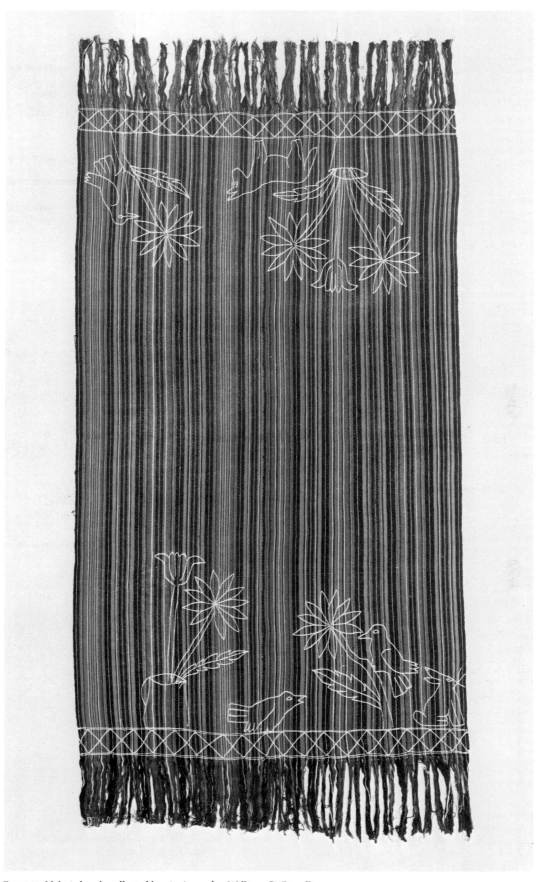

Fig. 141 Nebaj shawl, collected by Ambassador William G. Bowdler
in 1973. Cotton. 80 x 38½″ (2.03 x .98 m. including fringe).

Fig. 142 Nebaj tzute, collected by Lilly de Jongh Osborne (196), probably dating from the Thirties or Forties. Cotton and silk. 35¾ x 24″ (91 x 61 cm.).

Fig. 143 Nebaj tzute, collected by Mrs. F.R. Fisher in 1965-66. Cotton. 50 x 25½" (1.27 x .65 m.) (including fringe). Textile Museum 1973.11.6. Gift of Mrs. F.R. Fisher.

10. For example, Colby and Berghe 1969, pl. 19, and Bowdler 1981, cover; Anderson 1978, Figs. 97, 98, and Ordoñez and Paz 1975, p. 51.

11. Osborne's tag for the huipil in Fig. 133 gives a date of 1890; it is not clear on what basis the date was arrived at. It seems unlikely in view of the technical arguments presented here, as well as the similarity to examples in the 1942 photographs in the Carnegie Archive at the Peabody Museum.

12. This technique is described in detail by Sperlich 1980, pp. 154-59.

13. Wood and Osborne 1966, p. 88, indicate that in the late Thirties and early Forties the material used to bind up the women's hair was not standardized, and that strips of red cotton fabric, wool cords, or Totonicapán ribbons might be worn. The watercolor shows a red and white band, however, smaller than that now used, as do The National Geographic (Marden) photographs from 1945 (e.g., pl. VIII bottom). Crocker 1952 pl. 11 describes the hair band as 3" (7.5 cm.) wide, although the effect produced in his painting would require a wider one (it is put on as described here for the modern ones). In the black-and-white photographs published here it is difficult to be sure of the materials used. Today, virtually everyone wears the large hair band in the manner described here.

14. This description is based not only on the photographs shown here, but on my notes from watching a Nebaj woman do her hair twice, in demonstrations at the Textile Museum organized by Lydia Parks in 1981.

15. There is a shawl in the Eisen Collection (3-213) labelled as that of a man from Nebaj. It is two loom widths wide and has fringes on both ends, like the woman's shawls shown. It has dark blue and white warp stripes, each about ½" (1 cm.) wide.

16. See Martel c. 1975, p. 69.

17. The Nebaj tzute in the Eisen collection (O'Neale 1945, Fig. 114b) is labelled a man's headcloth, which it may possibly be, though the available photographs from the Forties and later do not show a man's headcloth. In pl. 13 in Colby and Berghe 1969, men in a cofradía, shown carrying the saint's image, have scarves tied under their chins, but the fabrics appear to be commercial and not handwoven. The modern tzutes are made by women for their own use. The Eisen tzute, and another example in the Heyde Collection (65/2095), are made in a size and format similar to the later ones, although without horizontal banding, and with the brocading technique partly comparable to the turn-of-the-century huipils and partly perhaps to the men's sashes.

18. See references in note 4.

REFERENCES

Ethnographic Photographs:
Marden 1945, pls. IV, XIV, market (color); pls. VIII (two photos), IX (top), women (color)
Colby and Berghe 1969, pl. 5, woman; pl. 6, house with woman weaving on the porch; pl. 9, children; pl. 11, crowd scene with cofradías; pl. 12, cofradía women; pl. 13 cofradía men; pl. 14, men and women at fiesta; pl. 15, municipal officials; pl. 19, woman
Ordoñez and Paz 1975, cover (color), p. 43, cofradía women; p. 39 (color), p. 47, market
Martel c. 1975, p. 69, woman with baby (color); p. 68 bottom, girls (color)
Bjerregaard 1977, p. 84, woman
Bunch 1977, p. vi, cofradía women (color)
Anderson 1978, p. 9 center left, woman
Sperlich 1980, p. xiii, mother and daughter; pp. xv, 85, young girl weaving; p. 71 top left, woman

Techniques:
Bjerregaard 1977, pp. 84-85, two-panel huipil
Anderson 1978, pp. 90-92, Figs. 97, 98, tzute and huipils
Sperlich 1980, pp. 134-36, three-panel huipil; pp. 150-53, two-panel huipil; p. 154-59, woman's belt

Textiles:
O'Neale 1945, Fig. 114b, Eisen Collection, man's tzute; Fig. 123b, c, Eisen collection, men's sashes
Osborne 1965, p. 42, 1975, p. 171, woman model (color)
Altman 1975, Fig. 14, two-panel huipil
Marks 1975, p. 5, third from right, belt
Anderson 1978, dust jacket (color), two-panel huipil (detail)
Heard 1979, p. 56 bottom, detail of huipil

Color Renderings:
Crocker 1952, pl. 11, women and man
Osborne 1965, pl. 70 right (1975, p. 253), woman; 1965, pl. 71 (1975, p. 255), man and woman cofrades
Wood and Osborne 1966, pl. 28, man; pl. 29, woman
Petterson 1977, pp. 60-61, no. 10, woman

Drawings:
Wood and Osborne 1966, p. 88, woman's belt
Ordoñez and Paz 1975, pp. 44-45, cofradía huipil; pp. 48-49, two-panel huipil; pp. 50-51, three-panel huipil

Text:
O'Neale 1945, p. 282, man's costume

Background:
Colby and Berghe 1969, emphasis on Indian-Ladino relations

Erroneous attribution:
Osborne 1965, pl. 29a, actually Cotzal (1975, p. 213)

CHAPTER TWELVE

San Mateo Ixtatán

Although San Mateo Ixtatán is even more remote than Todos Santos, its costume too was recorded and collected from early in the twentieth century. There are salt water springs in the area and the people gather the salt and export it. The population was nearly 9,000 in 1948. San Mateo is the only Chuj village with a costume that is documented.

The huipil is unlike the others discussed in that it is made of commercial cotton fabric, and not handwoven. It consists of two pieces of plain white fabric. One long piece is arranged sideways and the ends are sewn together to form a tube. This forms the lower part of the huipil. The upper part is formed of a piece half the length of the first, folded in half lengthwise, with its sides sewn to the tube of the lower part. A round hole is cut in the middle for the neck opening. The ends are partially sewn, leaving armholes.

In the earliest available examples, from the Twenties, the horizontal seam is covered by a band embroidered in red, and there is additional embroidery in concentric circles around the neck hole above the red band.[1] The character of this embroidery may be seen in the example illustrated in Color Plate XIII, although this piece has broader embroidery on it than do the earlier ones. The huipil illustrated here is transitional to the style found later in the Thirties (Figs. 144 and 145), since the neck embroidery has expanded to such an extent that the red band (now striped with yellow and green) is displaced from covering the seam. In this example, as well as in some of the earlier ones, the armholes are also framed by embroidery and there are small free-form embroidered birds, plants, and human figures below the neckline patterning.

Some of these early huipils are made of one layer of fabric, some of two layers, and some, as in the example in Color Plate XIII, of two layers above the seam but only one below. The embroidery stitches are large, passing back and forth across the entire width of each band. A false satin stitch is used, in which the needle catches only a small amount of fabric at the edge of the design between crossing the width of the pattern area on the front.[2] On the back, only the tiny stitches at the edges of the designs are visible. Red, yellow, and green cotton, pink wool, and a small amount of silk are used for the embroidery on the example in Color Plate XIII, and some narrow commercial braided wool tapes are also applied.

During the Thirties, the red band was abandoned and a series of six-pointed star shapes was added around the neckline. The photograph in Fig. 144, although not as clear as one might wish, shows this design in an early form, with the stars and their outlines still relatively simple.[3] The design extends about 18″ (46 cm.) from the shoulder, to below waist level. One of the huipils also has a small light-colored ruffle added to the neck.

The huipil in Fig. 145, though undated, is probably a later piece than the one in Fig. 144.[4] The embroidery has been expanded to cover 23½″ (60 cm.) from the shoulder line. Blue and white or green and white bands worked in double running stitch separate the broad red bands of false satin stitch. All of the embroidery is done in cotton yarns. This huipil is made of two layers of fabric throughout. Like the older examples, the embroidery appears only on the front, since it is worked in false satin stitch.

By the mid-Sixties, the embroidery had expanded to as broad as 30″ (76 cm.) from the shoulder, nearly the whole length of the huipil.[5] The examples in Figs. 146 and 147 give the general effect, although the huipil in figure 147 is a small-sized one, probably made for a child. The design is also more elaborate in these examples than in earlier ones. The two-color bands separating the broad red ones are wider and done with crosswise stitches, and may be zigzagged or serrated. Additional bands in pink or purple are used. The centers of the circles are filled with pattern. The use of a ruffled collar becomes more common and the collars are decorated with lace, ribbons, and rickrack.

Most of these later examples are made of two layers of fabric throughout, and, in addition, the design appears identically on both sides of the fabric. In at least some of these examples true satin stitch is used to create this effect. The heavy weight of the ground fabric and the addition of so much embroidery make the huipils very heavy, which is practical for the cold damp climate. The huipil is worn loose outside of the skirt, hanging to about knee length.

The skirt in the Twenties and Thirties was made of predominantly red, treadle-loom woven fabric, with narrow weft stripes in ikat (blue and white), yellow, and green.[6] It is not completely certain when the type of skirt fabric shown in Fig. 148 was introduced. It seems to have been used at least in the Sixties.[7] It is also treadle-loom woven, red with

Fig. 144 San Mateo Ixtatán women, 1935. Middle American Research Institute, Tulane University, Matilda Geddings Gray Collection.

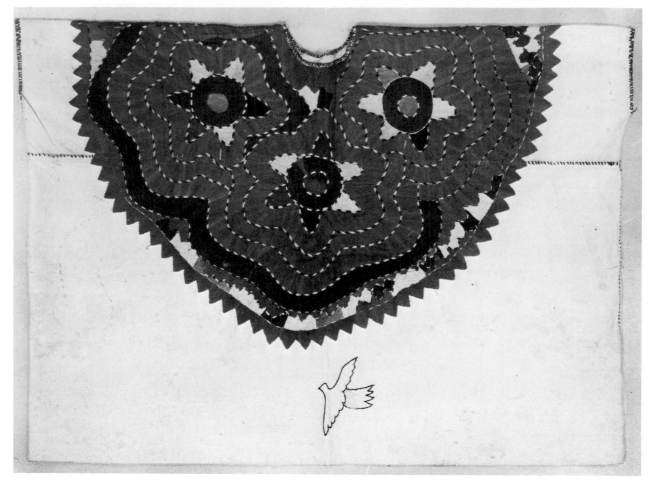

Fig. 145 San Mateo Ixtatán huipil, collected by Lilly de Jongh
Osborne (221), probably dating from the Forties or Fifties. Cotton.
31½ x 45¼ " (.80 x 1.15 m.).

narrow yellow weft stripes, and wider weftwise bands woven in simple plain-weave-derived float weaves in white, blue, green, and yellow. Today the usual skirt fabric is blue and green double ikat of the type woven in Salcajá (Fig. 89). The skirt is a rectangle, worn tightly wrapped, with the end tucked in at the waist rather than being secured with a belt.[8]

The hair style is arranged with the help of colored, commercial wool braid ribbons (Fig. 146). It is not clear from the available photographs exactly how it is done, but much of the mass rests on top of the head. When a scarf is worn, the height of the hairdress becomes even more striking. The photograph in Fig. 144 shows two ways of wearing the scarf, one with it tied under the chin, and one tied on the forehead (after folding the square into a triangle). Neither of these styles seems particularly common today, when the triangle is normally tied at the nape of the neck. Commercial fabric is used for the scarf. The two in Fig. 144 appear to be of relatively heavy cotton fabric, and bandannas were also often used. Today, rayon or syn-

thetic fabrics, some with floral prints, are common.

It is a curious fact that although all of the materials of the San Mateo Ixtatán women's costume are commercially produced rather than home-woven, and some are even machine-made, the actual manner of wearing the skirt, huipil, and hair seems to be directly descended from pre-Spanish antecedents.

NOTES

1. See LaFarge and Byers 1931, p. 35, Fig. 11e (MARI acc. no. 41-488). This huipil appears to be the same as the one of which there is a drawing in O'Neale (1945, Fig. 35a), although she seems not to have made the connection. The error of attribution is corrected in LaFarge 1947. He also describes this huipil as "somewhat less elaborate than average . . . the kind that would usually be made for an older child." It lacks the free-standing plant, bird, and human figure motifs found on other examples such as Color Plate XIII. A similar huipil, in the University Museum Collection, is published in Goodman 1976, p. 51 bottom (probably acc. no. 42-35-417). Other examples in the University Museum are one collected in 1915-1920 by Robert Burkitt (29-60-1) and another in the Osborne collection (42-35-416).

2. Elsewhere the stitch is described as satin stitch (e.g., by O'Neale 1945, p. 86; Goodman 1976, p. 51), in which the stitches are of equal length on the front and back of the fabric. This description is

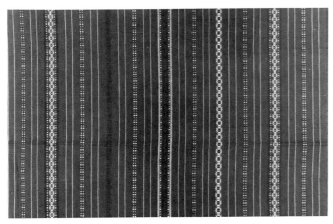

Fig. 148 San Mateo Ixtatán skirt fabric (detail showing half of loom width, warp horizontal), collected by Lilly de Jongh Osborne (122), probably dating from the Sixties. Cotton. Loom width: 33″ (84 cm.).

erroneous, at least for all these early examples.

3. The huipil worn by the woman on the right is now in the Gray collection at Tulane, and a drawing of it is published by O'Neale 1945, Fig. 38 (MARI 41-41a).

4. This huipil is illustrated in color in Osborne 1965, pl. 47 (1975, p. 180). The side shown is opposite to the one photographed for this catalogue.

5. A huipil made in 1965, in the collection of Marilyn Anderson, has a pattern of this size. The overall dimensions of this huipil are 33½″ (85 cm.) x 48″ (122 cm.). It is embroidered partly in false satin (red areas) and partly in true satin stitch (the two-color lines).

6. Described by LaFarge and Byers 1931, p. 36 and O'Neale 1945, p. 278. Delgado (1963, p. 168) describes the skirts of the Fifties as similar but with relatively wide white stripes, and some predominantly navy instead of red.

7. See Petterson 1977, no. 55, p. 235.

8. LaFarge and Byers 1931, p. 36; confirmed for San Mateo by Emily Norton. O'Neale (1945, p. 278) mentions a belt in the Gray Collection at Tulane. This is, however, of flimsy construction and not likely to be authentic everyday wear.

REFERENCES

Ethnographic Photographs:
Bunch 1977, p. 77, boy and girl (color)
Frost 1980, p. 31 top, woman embroidering (color)

Textiles:
LaFarge and Byers 1931, p. 35, Fig. 11e, huipil (Tulane)
Osborne 1965, pl. 47 (color) (1975, p. 180), huipil
Marks 1973, p. 6 (color), panel like huipil but no neck hole
Goodman 1976, p. 51 (bottom), pre-1930 huipil (UM); p. 48 (bottom), recent huipil (UM)
Anderson 1978, p. 179, Fig. 201 (bottom), detail of neck area

Color Renderings:
LaFarge and Byers 1931, plate opp. p. 36, woman (see comment in LaFarge 1947, pp. 166-67)
Petterson 1977, pp. 234-35, no. 55, woman

Drawings:
O'Neale 1945, Figs. 35a, 38, 42b, huipils; Fig. 52g, skirt fabric

Text:
LaFarge and Byers 1931, pp. 215, 225-26
O'Neale 1945, pp. 123, 130, 278, Tulane specimens
LaFarge 1947
Delgado, 1963, pp. 307-08, 1957 costume

Fig. 146 San Mateo Ixtatán woman, 1978. Photograph by Susan Masuoka; black and white from color original.

Fig. 147 San Mateo Ixtatán child's huipil, collected by Ruben Reina in 1970. Cotton. 23 x 32″ (59 x 81 cm.). University Museum, University of Pennsylvania 70-13-33.

CHAPTER THIRTEEN
Epilogue

The changes chronicled in this catalogue that have taken place in Guatemalan textiles over the last century are varied. Some of them seem natural and logical internally, such as the changes in the double-headed bird on Chichicastenango huipils up until 1960. Others are borrowings from neighboring towns, primarily from towns in which some textiles are commercially produced, such as the animal and chevron designs that Palín seems to have borrowed from San Pedro Sacatepéquez, the ikat shawls and sashes that Santiago Atitlán seems to have borrowed from San Pedro la Laguna, or the bird and vase designs that San Martín Sacatepéquez seems to have borrowed from Quezaltenango or another town under Quezaltenango influence. Also found is the exchange of one commercial product for another, as is occurring with the use of ikat instead of blue plaid fabric for skirts in some towns. Relatively few are directly attributable to

European influence, as is the case for the naturalistic floral designs of Chichicastenango, or the wearing of a blouse under the huipil as is now common in San Juan Sacatepéquez. There are even a few instances of a handwoven product being substituted for machine made fabric, as occurs in Todos Santos men's shirts.

The amount of technical innovation, within native textile traditions, is rather startling, considering the small number of towns covered and the short span of time involved. There is not only simplification, such as is found in Chichicastenango weaving, and what appears to be direct borrowing from other towns, such as occurs in Palín, but also what appear to be unprecedented technical systems, as in the new style of supplementary-weft patterning in Santiago Atitlán, and the more subtly different ways of producing the traditional design repertory that has occurred not once, but twice, in Nebaj. The scale of these changes helps us to understand how Guatemalan weaving became so rich and varied in the first place. It is possible that the slowness of the weaving process on the backstrap loom not only is conducive to work of artistic quality but also stimulates such technical innovations.

Plainly, the time has come to cease thinking of each town's style as a coherent unity, subject only to degeneration from European influences. It is easy, overwhelming as are the obvious regional distinctions in Guatemalan textiles, to understand how most people and most publications focus primarily on these distinctions. But the changes within individual towns have occurred at such a rate that unless such an approach is narrowly defined in time, the result is a misleading oversimplification.

It is tempting to those visiting Guatemala in recent years to consider the changes that have taken place in the Sixties and Seventies as some kind of degeneration from the "traditional" or "classic" style of the Thirties, a period in which the textiles were relatively well documented and published and so forming an accessible point of comparison. However, a more detailed investigation, going farther back in time, indicates that significant changes also occurred in many towns between 1910 and 1930. Embroidery was added to Santiago Atitlán huipils where there had been none before; the design repertory of Palín weaving was greatly expanded; a surface brocading technique began to be used on Nebaj huipils, and so on. Which style is then more "traditional"? We may admit that the textiles of the Thirties, with their lavish silks, appeal more directly to European or North American taste than either the earlier simpler and more restrained styles or the later more flamboyant ones, but it is not fair to say that one is more "traditional" than the other.

The changes in Guatemalan weaving documented in this catalogue constitute only the tip of an iceberg. One could, on the one hand, extend the examples from any of the towns covered. A dozen or more huipils from a single town could easily be illustrated without undue repetition. Further searches of textile and photographic collections would fill in the gaps in the documentation. It would also be well worthwhile to attempt to answer some of the questions raised by doing field work, especially to find out how some of the more striking changes took place. On the other hand, one could extend the investigation to other towns. There are many of equal interest to those discussed here, and some of them may have traditions that are complementary to others.

Some guidelines may be suggested for future students and collectors which will greatly aid this type of research. Most obvious is the simple process of keeping records of when photographs were taken and when individual textiles were collected, and whether a textile was new or old when bought, especially if material is accumulated over a span of several years. These dates should be included in any publication of the material, especially if textiles or photographs of different dates are included in the same publication. Field work done at a specific time should not be complemented by reference to textile collections made earlier (or later) unless possible differences are kept clearly in mind.

About the future of Guatemalan textiles, it is naturally risky to predict. In his 1924 article, Popenoe predicted an imminent decline of Guatemalan textiles which, in view of how rich the Thirties were in textile activity, makes one wary. Ordinarily, there might not be any special cause for alarm, although overall acculturation is taking place in some areas and various specific factors have been cited as causes of decline. The increasing pressure to produce goods for sale to tourists has caused some loss of quality since speed becomes a factor when weaving has a commercial rather than domestic end, although the slowness of backstrap loom weaving is not a disadvantage when the end product will be used rather than sold. The earthquake of 1976 caused so much damage in some towns that people have had to concentrate their resources and energies on basic necessities rather than art. These factors, however, are insignificant beside the current escalating violence, in which the native people must fear for their very lives. It is the outcome of this struggle that will determine the survival of native Guatemalan culture.

Bibliography

Altman, Patricia B., and Raúl López
1975   *Guatemala: Quetzal and Cross.* Exhibition organized by the UCLA Museum of Cultural History, Sept. 28–Dec. 14, 1975. Frederick S. Wight Art Galleries, University of California at Los Angeles.

Anawalt, Patricia Rieff
1975   *Pan-Mesoamerican Costume Repertory at the Time of Spanish Contact.* Ph.D. dissertation. University of California at Los Angeles, Department of Anthropology.

Anderson, Marilyn
1978   *Guatemalan Textiles Today.* Watson-Guptill, New York.

Atwater, Mary M.
1954   *Byways in Handweaving.* Macmillan, New York.
1965   *Guatemala Visited.* 1946 ed. reprinted as Shuttle Craft Monograph 15. Lansing, MI.

Bird, Junius
1953   "Two Guatemalan Wedding Huipils." *Bulletin of the Needle and Bobbin Club,* vol. 37, nos. 1-2: 27-36. New York.

Bjerregaard, Lena
1977   *Techniques of Guatemalan Weaving.* Van Nostrand Reinhold, New York.

Borhegyi, Stephan F. de
1965   "Archaeological Synthesis of the Guatemalan Highlands." *Handbook of Middle American Indians,* vol. 2, pp. 3-58. University of Texas Press, Austin.

Bowdler, Ann
1981   *Guatemalan Art: The Bowdler Collection.* Exhibition, April 24–May 11, Northern Virginia Community College, Alexandria.

Breuer, Alice Putnam
1942   *Guatemalan Textiles: Prentiss N. Gray Collection.* Mills College Art Gallery, Oakland, Ca.

Bunch, Roland, and Roger Bunch
1977   *The Highland Maya: Patterns of Life and Clothing in Indian Guatemala.* Josten's Publications, Visalia, Ca.

Bunzel, Ruth
1952   *Chichicastenango: A Guatemalan Village.* American Ethnological Society. Publication 22. (Reprinted 1959, 3rd printing 1967, University of Washington Press.)

Bunzl, George
1966   *The Face of the Sun Kingdoms.* Fountain Press Ltd. (1st American edition, 1969, A. S. Barnes and Co., South Brunswick and New York.)

Carnegie Institution of Washington
1935   "Textile Arts of the Guatemalan Natives." *News Service Bulletin,* February 3, vol. III, no. 20, pp. 157-168.

Colby, Benjamin N., and Pierre L. van den Berghe
1969   *Ixil Country.* University of California Press, Berkeley and Los Angeles.

Crocker, Frederick J.
1952   *Trajes de Guatemala.* 2 vols. Editorial B. Zadik y Cia., Guatemala.

Delgado, Hildegard Schmidt de
(see also Pang, Hilda Delgado)

1963 *Aboriginal Guatemalan Handweaving and Costume.* Ph.D. dissertation, Indiana University, Department of Anthropology. University Microfilms 64-459, Ann Arbor.

1968a "Figurines of Backstrap Loom Weavers from the Maya Area." *Verhandlungen des XXXVIII Internationalen Amerikanisten-Kongresses,* Band I, pp. 139-149. Kommissionsverlag Klaus Renner, Munich.

1968b "Guatemalan Indian Handweaving: Conservatism and Change in a Village Handicraft." *Verhandlungen des XXXVIII Internationalen Amerikanisten-Kongresses,* Band II, pp. 449-457. Kommissionsverlag Klaus Renner, Munich.

Dutton, Bertha
1939 "All Saints' Day Ceremonies in Todos Santos, Guatemala." *El Palacio,* no. 46, pp. 169-182, 205-217. Santa Fe.

Emery, Irene
1966 *The Primary Structures of Fabrics.* The Textile Museum, Washington, D.C.

Fay, Howard La
1975 "The Maya, Children of Time." *National Geographic,* vol. 148, no. 6, December, pp. 728-767. Washington, D.C.

Frost, Gordon
1980 "Guatemala: Weaving, People." *Interweave,* Vol. V, no. 4, pp. 30-32. Loveland, Colo.

Gayer, Jacob
1926 "In the Land of the Quetzal." *The National Geographic Magazine,* vol. L, no. 5, November, pp. 610-627. Washington, D.C.

Goodman, Frances
1976 *The Embroidery of Mexico and Guatemala.* Charles Scribner's Sons, New York.

Grossman, Ellin F.
1955 "Textiles and Looms from Guatemala and Mexico." *Handweaver and Craftsman,* vol. 7, no. 1, Winter 1955-56, pp. 6-11.

Haba, Louis de la
1974 "Guatemala, Maya and Modern." *National Geographic,* vol. 146, no. 5, November, pp. 660-689. Washington, D.C.

Handbook of Middle American Indians
1967 Vol. 6, Social Anthropology.
1969 Vols. 7-8, Ethnology. Robert Wauchope, ed. University of Texas Press, Austin.

Heard Museum
1979 *Guatemalan Costumes.* Text by Mary G. Dieterich, Jon T. Erickson, and Erin Younger. Phoenix.

Kelsey, Vera, and Lilly de Jongh Osborne
1939 *Four Keys to Guatemala.* Revised Edition 1961, Funk and Wagnalls.

Lafarge, Oliver, II, and Douglas Byers
1931 *The Year Bearer's People.* Tulane University of Louisiana, Middle American Research Series Publication no. 3, New Orleans.

LaFarge, Oliver, II
1947 "Cuchumatán Textiles: The Course of an Error." *Notes on Middle American Archaeology and Ethnology,* no. 82, October 13, pp. 166-169. Carnegie Institution of Washington, Division of Historical Research.

Lee, Thomas F.
1926 "Guatemala: Land of Volcanoes and Progress. Cradle of Ancient Mayan Civilization, Redolent with Its Later Spanish and Indian Ways, Now Reaping Prosperity from Bananas and Coffee." *The National Geographic Magazine,* vol. L, no. 5, November, pp. 599-648, Washington, D.C.

Lehmann, Henri
1961 "Exposition: Costumes Maya d'Aujourd'hui." *Objets et Mondes,* vol. 1, part 1, pp. 3-32. Paris, Musée de l'Homme.

Lemos, Pedro José
1941 *Guatemala Art Crafts.* Worcester, Mass.: Davis Press.

Liebler, Barbara
1980 "In the Beginning." *Interweave,* vol. 5, no. 4, Fall, pp. 52-54. Loveland, Col.

Long, John E.
1936 "Guatemala Interlude: In the Land of the Quetzal a Modern Capital Contrasts with Primitive Indian Villages and the 'Pompeii of America.'" *The National Geographic Magazine,* vol. LXX, no. 4, October, pp. 429-460. Washington, D.C.

Lothrop, Samuel K.
1928a "Santiago Atitlán, Guatemala." Museum of the American Indian, Heye Foundation, *Indian Notes,* vol. 5, no. 4.
1928b Notes on Guatemalan Textiles. MS in Peabody Museum Library.

Mahler, Joy
1965 "Garments and Textiles of the Maya Lowlands." *Handbook of Middle American Indians,* vol. 3, pp. 581-593. University of Texas Press, Austin.

Marden, Luis
36 "Where Man's Garb Rivals the Quetzal." *The National Geographic Magazine,* vol. LXX, no. 4, October, pp. 437-444, Washington, D.C.
1945 "To Market in Guatemala." *The National Geographic Magazine,* vol. LXXVIII, no. 1, July, pp. 87-104, Washington, D.C.
1947 "Guatemala Revisited." *The National Geographic Magazine,* vol. LXXXII, no. 4, October, pp. 525-564, Washington, D.C.

Marks, Copeland H.
1973 "In Pursuit of the Elusive Huipil." *Handweaver and Craftsman,* vol. 24, no. 4, pp. 6-9.
1975 "The Guatemalan Weaver." *Handweaver and Craftsman,* vol. 26, no. 5, October, pp. 2-6.
1976 "Three Men's Costumes: Weaving of the Guatemalan Highland Maya." *Shuttle, Spindle, and Dyepot,* no. 28, Fall, pp. 88-91.

Martel, Olivier (photographs)
c.1975 *Guatemala.* Text by Ph. Bordas and J.P. Gagnere. Editions Debroisse, Boulogne.

Maudslay, Anne Carey, and
Alfred Percival Maudslay
1899   *A Glimpse at Guatemala, and some notes on the Ancient Monuments of Central America.* John Murray, London.

McBryde, Felix Webster
1947   *Cultural and Historical Geography of Southwest Guatemala.* Smithsonian Institution, Institute of Social Anthropology, publication no. 4. Washington, D.C.

Mendelson, E. Michael
1958   "A Guatemalan Sacred Bundle." *Man,* no. 58, art. 170, pp. 121-126.

Muñoz, Joaquín, and Anna Bell Ward
1940   *Guatemala Ancient and Modern.* Pyramid Press, New York.

Oakes, Maud
1951a   *The Two Crosses of Todos Santos: Survivals of Maya Religious Festivals.* Bollingen series no. 27.
1951b   *Beyond the Windy Place: Life in the Guatemalan Highlands.* New York.

O'Neale, Lila M.
1945   *Textiles of Highland Guatemala.* Carnegie Institution of Washington, publication no. 567.

Ordoñez, David, and Arturo Paz
1975   *Algo de los Ixiles.* El Dzunun, Guatemala.

Osborne, Lilly de Jongh
1935   *Guatemalan Textiles.* Tulane University of Louisiana, Middle American Research Series publication no. 6. New Orleans.
1965   *Indian Crafts of Guatemala and El Salvador.* University of Oklahoma Press, Norman. Second Edition, 1975.

Pancake, Cherri M.
1976   *The Costumes of Rural Guatemala: An Exhibit Guide.* Museo Ixchel del Traje Indigena, Guatemala.

Pang, Hilda Delgado
(see also Delgado, Hildegard Schmidt de)
1977a   "A Preliminary Bibliography on Guatemalan Ethnographic Textiles." In *Irene Emery Roundtable on Museum Textiles, 1976 Proceedings, Ethnographic Textiles of the Western Hemisphere,* pp. 94-105, Irene Emery and Patricia Fiske, eds. The Textile Museum, Washington, D.C.
1977b   "Similarities Between Certain Early Spanish, Contemporary Spanish Folk, and Mesoamerican Indian Textile Design Motifs." op. cit. pp. 386-404.

Petterson, Carmen L.
1977   *The Maya of Guatemala: Their Life and Dress.* Ixchel Museum, Guatemala City/University of Washington Press, Seattle and London.

Popenoe, Wilson
1924   "Regional Differences in the Guatemalan Huipil." *Annaes do XX Congresso Internacional de Americanistas,* vol. 1, pp. 217-220. Rio de Janeiro.

Reina, Ruben E., and Robert M. Hill, II
1978   *The Traditional Pottery of Guatemala.* University of Texas Press, Austin.

Ricketson, O.G.
1939   "Municipal organization of an Indian township of Guatemala." *Geographic Review,* no. 29, pp. 643-647.

Rodas, N. Flavio and C. Ovidio Rodas
1938   *Simbolismos (Maya Quichés) de Guatemala.* Guatemala.

Rodas, Flavio, C. Ovidio Rodas and
Laurence F. Hawkins
1940   *Chichicastenango: The Kiche Indians, Their History and Culture, Sacred Symbols of Their Dress and Textiles.* Unión Tipográfica, Guatemala.

Scofield, John
1960   "Easter Week in Indian Guatemala." *National Geographic,* vol. 117, no. 3, March, pp. 406-417, Washington, D.C.

Siskin, Barbara
1977   "Changes in Woven Design from Santo Tomás Chichicastenango." In *Irene Emery Roundtable on Museum Textiles, 1976 Proceedings, Ethnographic Textiles of the Western Hemisphere,* pp. 154-158. Irene Emery and Patricia Fiske, eds. The Textile Museum, Washington, D.C.

Sowards, Elizabeth Willis
1974   *The Guatemalan Huipil.* Gallery Guide. The Textile Museum, Washington, D.C.

Sperlich, Norbert, and
Elizabeth Katz Sperlich
1980   *Guatemalan Backstrap Weaving.* University of Oklahoma Press, Norman.

Start, Laura E.
1948   *The McDougall Collection of Indian Textiles from Guatemala and Mexico.* Pitt Rivers Museum, University of Oxford Occasional Papers on Technology, no. 2. Oxford University Press.

Tulane
1976   *Traditional Indian Costume of Guatemala.* Entries by Ann W. Bowdler and Lucy Leonowens; introduction by Sue Woodward. Middle American Research Institute, Tulane University, New Orleans.

Wood, Josephine, and Lilly de Jongh Osborne
1966   *Indian Costumes of Guatemala.* Akademische Druck- und Verlagsanstalt, Graz.

Young, Helen Daniels
1953   "Adventures with Guatemalan Weaving." *Hand-Weaver and Craftsman,* vol. 4, no. 1, Winter, pp. 26-29, 47-49.